Succeeding as a History Teacher

Succeeding as a History Teacher

EMILY FOLORUNSHO
WITH
LAURA GLADWIN

BLOOMSBURY EDUCATION
LONDON OXFORD NEW YORK NEW DELHI SYDNEY

BLOOMSBURY EDUCATION
Bloomsbury Publishing Plc
50 Bedford Square, London, WC1B 3DP, UK
29 Earlsfort Terrace, Dublin 2, Ireland

BLOOMSBURY, BLOOMSBURY EDUCATION and the Diana logo are
trademarks of Bloomsbury Publishing Plc

First published in Great Britain 2024 by Bloomsbury Publishing Ltd

This edition published in Great Britain 2024 by Bloomsbury Publishing Ltd

A catalogue record for this book is available from the British Library

ISBN: PB: 978-1-8019-9221-3; ePDF: 978-1-8019-9219-0;
ePub: 978-1-8019-9222-0

2 4 6 8 10 9 7 5 3 1 (paperback)

Typeset by Newgen KnowledgeWorks Pvt. Ltd., Chennai, India
Printed and bound in the UK by CPI Group (UK) Ltd., Croydon, CR0 4YY

To find out more about our authors and books visit www.bloomsbury.com
and sign up for our newsletters.

Contents

PART 3: Developing yourself

Acknowledgements

The authors would like to thank the teachers who have so kindly shared their experiences and insights in the case studies within this resource: Sian Ayling, Martyn Bajkowski, Ashley Bartlett, Jen Brown, Sally Burnham, Elizabeth Carr, Rebecca Chadwick, Rachel Cliffe, Harriet Cornwell, Rosie Culkin-Smith, Natasha De Stefano Honey, Fiona Gambles, Alex Gordon, Swerupa Gosrani, Kyle Graham, Andy Hassan, Dr Simon Henderson, Tom Hopkins Burke, Sophie Hudson, Ammar Khan, Jema Kinsman, Hannah McInroy-Betts, Jonathan Mountstevens, Chloe Oliver, Patrick O'Shaughnessy, Lindsey Rawes, Claire Sargeant, Kristian Shanks and Laura Tarantini-Amor.

Special thanks to Emmanuel. Without you, I would have given up. Thank you for always being there and helping me; I appreciate you deeply. Thank you to my mum, who has sacrificed for me to be where I am today; I am a product of her sacrifice. Thank you to Joanna Ramsay, for all her patience and help in the process. Thank you to my colleagues over the years and the history Twitter community for helping me to improve my practice. Finally, thank you to my students, old, present and future. You have been my greatest teachers.

Emily Folorunsho

I would like to dedicate my sections of this book to my family, who have always given their full support. Thank you to Mum, Dad, Jon, James, Emma, Grandma and Grandad. In particular, this book is in memory of my late grandfather Pete, who always reminded me of my childhood dream of writing a book.

Laura Gladwin

Foreword

To be a teacher of history is a privilege. We pass on our passion, knowledge and insight about the past to future generations. From key events to significant individuals, examining historical sources, assessing change and continuity to storytelling, history is a truly special subject. Through learning about the past, we can gain a greater understanding of the present day.

Although it is an absolute joy to be a history teacher, it is not without its obstacles. There are challenging conversations that must take place about curriculum content, breadth versus depth and the vast amount of content that teachers are expected to teach and students are expected to be able to recall from long term memory. This book helps the history teacher to overcome these barriers to succeed as a history teacher.

Emily Folorunsho and Laura Gladwin bring enthusiasm, experience and expertise to this wonderful book. The authors draw on evidence available as well as sharing advice and guidance from their own classroom experiences and reflections. The authors demonstrate an ability to apply evidence to the classroom whilst always providing a subject-specific focus and lens.

The history curriculum is often driven by chronology. This makes sense, as it helps students to develop an understanding of the passage of time and have an awareness of key developments and events that have often shaped culture, traditions and the political landscape. However, knowing what to include – and exclude – can be complex and multifaceted. Difficult decisions about exam specifications and course content also contribute to the overall curriculum plan. This book tackles areas linked to curriculum from choosing the historical content, considering the design and assessment process and outcomes as well as ensuring students have access to a knowledge-rich and diverse curriculum.

Following on from curriculum conversations is a chapter heavily rooted in research with plentiful advice and guidance about lesson planning, always with the history context at the core. From storytelling to feedback, essential elements of teaching and learning in the history classroom are explored and accompanied with practical examples.

The final chapter of the book is relevant for every history teacher, and middle or senior leader, as it focuses on continual professional learning and development. Developing our subject knowledge, expertise and confidence should be ongoing. As all history teachers know, like our students, we too have gaps in our knowledge that we need to be aware of so we can therefore close those gaps. We also have areas of strength that we should share with our colleagues and the wider history community.

This book will become essential reading from the trainee history teacher to the more experienced classroom teacher to the head of history and senior line managers supporting history departments. I encourage the reader to revisit this book regularly, reflect, discuss it with colleagues and enjoy putting the practical advice into practice in the classroom.

Kate Jones

Senior Associate for Teaching and Learning at Evidence Based Education, teacher of history and former head of history.

Introduction

Succeeding as a History Teacher has been written to provide a wealth of practical ideas for you as a history teacher in developing a coherent and diverse curriculum, delivering effective lessons, building your subject knowledge and growing in your career. We do not expect that you will read it in one go but instead have designed it so that you can dip in and out of it as a reference.

We have divided the book into three distinct sections, to help with navigation: part 1 focuses on building your curriculum and assessment; part 2 looks at principles and practical strategies for delivering effective history lessons; and part 3 focuses on you and your development.

Chapter 5 on developing historical knowledge and skills is written by Laura Gladwin and Chapter 9 on supporting all students is written with Laura Tarantini-Amor. All other chapters are written by Emily Folorunsho.

Each chapter guides you through a specific theme, drawing on research, and provides realistic, practical strategies to use in the classroom. There are case studies in most chapters, offering insights from teachers in a range of contexts.

Online resource centre

Where appropriate, we provide templates and resources that you can use in your own planning and teaching. Downloadable versions of templates and further case studies are available on the online resource centre: www.bloomsbury.pub/Succeeding-History-Teacher

We hope you enjoy this book and find it useful in your teaching and career.

PART 1

Thinking about your history curriculum

1

Choosing the content

In this chapter, I explore a starting point for your secondary history teaching: choosing the content for your history curriculum. We discuss developing a vision for your curriculum with your department that is bespoke to your students and school community, and using that vision to inform your curriculum topic choices.

The purpose of history education

Choosing what students will learn is a huge responsibility, and it is influenced by many factors. One of these is our own beliefs about the purposes of history education. For some, the most important aspect is developing a sense of identity; for others, it is about the transferable skills that students can take forward to their future lives. The National Curriculum (DfE, 2013) states that 'History helps pupils to understand the complexity of people's lives, the process of change, the diversity of societies and relationships between different groups, as well as their own identity and the challenges of their time.' In essence, there are many purposes for teaching history; therefore, it is important that as a department you discuss what you each believe to be key, to get a good idea of what is important for everybody. Your collective priorities can then underpin your selection of content and pedagogy. With the time constraints imposed on us, we cannot necessarily fit everything we would want to teach into a curriculum. Therefore, having your vision clear as a department will enable you to make hard choices on what to include and what to leave out.

Your departmental vision

Here is an example of my department's vision:

Belong

- To deliver a representative curriculum which enables students to see themselves and understand others in our globalised world.

- To enable our students to gain cultural capital but also cultural confidence in their own identities and stories.

- To develop an understanding of how history informs our sense of identity and place in the world through studying a range of periods, perspectives and peoples.

- To develop a passion for history, a respect and understanding for all people and deeper understanding of the human spirit.

- To empower our students as they interact with both their intellect and identities.

Aspire

- To introduce students to stories and knowledge that will create aspirations within them to reach their potential and make a difference in their communities.

- To support students to aspire to great career paths through our history graduate network. (This network is a team of successful graduates in various industries including medicine, finance consultancy, law and STEM. The network is designed to show career progression from history GCSE and A level to degree level and beyond.)

Succeed

- For students to make progress academically by focusing on literacy and transferable analytical skills and critical thinking.

- To impart skills and knowledge that will enable students to succeed in the wider world and chosen careers.

Academic rigour and disciplinary knowledge

- To support the disciplinary knowledge of history through our curriculum, and for all our enquiries to be rooted in the use of sources and academic scholarship.

Self-development

- To develop a greater sense of self and the critical importance of historical literacy to navigate the present and the future.

- To be energised and empowered by our curriculum choices: history should nourish and develop students' intellect, cultural competence and critical consciousness.

- To offer enrichment opportunities to build cultural capital and foster students' exploration of their wider community beyond their home city, as well as exposing them to the richness of local histories.

Choosing content to meet your vision

After building your departmental vision, you then need to choose the content. Ask yourself: 'What is the most powerful knowledge that meets our vision for history in *this* school?' (See Chapter 5 for more on 'powerful knowledge'.) This will make it easier to select the content and frame your enquiries. You may agree or disagree with the specific ideas in my school's vision above; however, you will hopefully see that it is centred on the needs of *our* students and wider community. Create your vision to serve the interests and development of your students and remember that it will change over time to suit evolving needs.

What to include/what not to include

In 2018, I attended Richard Kennett's workshop on revising his Key Stage 3 (KS3) curriculum at the West London Free School history teaching conference. He spoke about the ways in which we should choose and *not* choose content, which I have summarised below.

How to choose your content

- It enables students to make sense of the present day.
- It is a topic your team believe every student should learn.
- It helps students to understand their local community.
- It reflects what history academics are studying.
- It provides context for students' later studies.
- It builds on KS1 and KS2.

How *not* to choose your content

- It is engaging (but that is the only reason).
- It is gory and so has entertainment value.
- It has amusing stories from social history.
- It is a GCSE topic you could fit into KS3 to help with time pressures in KS4.
- It is what you have always done.
- You need to do a source unit and you have some sources for this topic.
- It will be easy to assess. (Richard Kennett, 2018)

Choosing content at KS3

I work in a non-academy school and the National Curriculum, alongside our student body, is our starting point for choosing content. The National Curriculum is a good starting point. It sets out broad expectations of what students will study yet allows flexibility to create something bespoke for your own community.

It is important to bear in mind that some of your students will stop studying history at the end of KS3. Therefore, you need to consider what you want these students to know and which values you want them to have fulfilled. Other students will study history at GCSE and beyond. For them, you need to decide what foundational knowledge they need to be able to navigate KS4 and KS5 effectively.

At the time of writing, my school is preparing for a three-year KS3 course. This means we are redesigning our Year 9 curriculum. As you will see below, various factors were relevant when selecting content. Here are some of the topics we chose and our rationale:

1. **British Empire through time:** We chose this as it is foundational knowledge needed for our migration course at KS4. We need students to encounter key words such as 'colonisation', 'colony', 'independence', etc. These are words they will see again in our KS4 course when studying Queen Elizabeth and migration. We also believe that this topic is important in its own right.

2. **Revolution through time and the Cold War:** We chose these as they introduce concepts such as communism that students need to come across before KS4 and KS5.

3. **The USA 1920–45:** We chose this to aid students that may choose to study history at KS5, because they will study civil rights in the USA 1865–1992 and, in order to be successful, they need to have a strong chronological understanding of the country's history. Previously, when teaching this KS5 course, I would often begin with a timeline lesson, and I was surprised by how little students knew about US history. Furthermore, this period is rich with various types of sources and therefore gives us scope to develop source skills.

4. **British civil rights, including rights for women, for people with disabilities and for Asian people living in Britain:** We chose this topic to build upon the civil rights in the USA course studied in Year 8 and prepare students for the similar course in KS5, as well as to prepare them for the migration unit in KS4.

Choosing content at KS4

At KS4, you need to choose content that will build upon students' KS3 learning whilst preparing them for KS5. You may want to consider teacher specialism and available resources when making these choices, but these should not be the most important factors. In our department, for example, we decided to move from teaching crime and punishment to teaching migration, as we believed that it had important content for our students to learn. None of us were specialists in the topic and there were few resources available, but we did have the textbook and found some helpful continuing professional development (CPD) events. Despite the obstacles, we changed the course content to better fulfil our departmental vision.

Choosing content at KS5

I do not believe that topics should be solely chosen due to teacher specialism or confidence, as this has often been used as a justification for not teaching diverse topics, especially at KS3. However, because in-depth subject knowledge is needed at KS5, keep teacher specialism in mind. Student interest and their contextual knowledge are also relevant factors at this stage.

BUILDING A CURRICULUM ON THE VERY BEST KNOWLEDGE

Harriet Cornwell, @knowledge_witch and @BeBoldHistory

What topics will you teach? What diet is your current curriculum founded on and what, in your mind, constitutes the 'very best knowledge' for your students in their context?

I have worked in two contrasting school contexts: the first a community that was predominantly White working class, and the second a school that had a vibrant international community. In both situations, the curricula I inherited almost entirely consisted of collections of knowledge that were heavily influenced by White British history. For students who came from an international background, their frustrations were levelled at the lack of representation of their home country on the curriculum, with their only experience being linked to colonial history of empire. Students who came from a working-class background found their frustrations in curriculum repeats, whereby they repeatedly studied, across KS2, KS3 and KS4, traditional topics such as the Battle of Hastings, the Tudors and World War Two on a seemingly endless loop.

What, then, constitutes students accessing the very best knowledge? Quite simply, following the National Curriculum for history does not justify your curriculum decisions in a robust or rigorous manner. This also does not always provide students with a broad scope of history; if you follow only the suggested topics, there is a danger that the subject of history ends up being associated with predominantly British or European histories. It can therefore provide a very narrow view of our subject and consequently we reproduce, with varying degrees of difficulty, the same knowledge.

Professor Peter Frankopan, author of *The Silk Roads: A New History of the World* (2016), talks in the preface about having a large map of the world in his bedroom and gradually becoming aware of the very restricted geographic focus of his learning at school.

This resonated with me for a long time. I imagined a map of the world where half of the history of the world had been left in dark, uncharted waters and censored by the dominant view of British, European and US histories. This personal experience from such a highly regarded and respected scholar fostered the need to build, design and write a curriculum that embraced the many narratives and histories captured in imagination through the history of the Silk Roads. This is it; this is our hook to entice Year 7 onto their curriculum journey. However, where should your curriculum voyage start? Does it begin with people, trade, travel, technology or time?

This is where the frustrations, dilemmas and professional wrestling of the curriculum leader and department begin. Yes, this does mean that we will be abandoning some of our tried and tested topics that we are used to teaching. Yes, it means that we will be at times out of our subject knowledge depth, but this liberating experience of sequencing knowledge that is new, exciting and global is a journey that is full of joy.

Because Peter Frankopan's book is such a ground-breaking piece of work, which challenges assumptions about where humans came from and what has shaped our history, our department unashamedly used the framework of the book to influence our curriculum thinking. Using the formation of the Silk Roads as our curriculum anchor – our point where we set sail – enabled us to use the chapter headings in the book to start to pencil in and sketch out a curriculum that would incorporate global, European and British histories as its rationale for curriculum design.

Naturally, we did not just keep to this one grand narrative when constructing our curriculum. Other books and scholarship allowed our sequencing to cover a scope of breadth as well as depth. Driven chronologically, our Year 7 curriculum is anchored to the Silk Roads, before travelling to the Arabian Peninsula, cruising to cities such as Baghdad and Constantinople, before meandering back to Britain on Viking longships.

Just because we have new and exciting histories on our curriculum does not mean that we have committed key turning points in British history to – please forgive me – the history books. Agreeing on essential knowledge from a British perspective is something for your departments to heavily debate. For me, topics like 1066 and the English Reformation are essential knowledge and should not be removed from your curriculum.

Once you start this process of curriculum reading, thinking and planning, you will find that your curriculum begins to grow and develop organically. You will find that the more you and your department read, research and write, the more 'golden threads' begin to emerge between topics. This is not to say that each carefully sequenced unit of work will naturally bind itself to the next; sometimes the routes you take will knot together knowledge for students' future learning, potentially out of the key stage in which they are studying.

Building a curriculum is not about plotting alternative histories over essential knowledge. Instead, it is about carefully constructing your curriculum, thinking strategically about what constitutes 'the very best knowledge'. The 'maiden voyage' will be the first test. However, this is the beauty of curriculum design. Debates around knowledge, e.g. 'Why this knowledge?' or 'Why teach it now?', are arguments that your department should never stop having. Why? Because history is never finished. Historians ask new and different questions about the past and we look to them to shape our thinking. This discipline is never final; it is always contested. Seek the most powerful knowledge (see Chapter 5), find courage and plot out the best knowledge for students in our schools.

Summary

- Consider how you and your team view the purpose of history education and together devise a shared vision for a history curriculum to suit the needs of your students and school community.

- Keep your vision at the heart of your content choices.

- All learning, and therefore all lessons, must link into your vision.

- Plan a balanced and broad curriculum, considering how the learning in different key stages can support and build on each other.

- Move away from your own areas of expertise in KS3 and KS4 where needed, to ensure that your vision is met, but draw on this expertise in KS5 to give your students the best insights possible.

2

Curriculum design and assessment

The previous chapter discussed choosing content for your history curriculum. In this chapter, I will explore how to develop those content choices into designing your complete history curriculum. We will start with a case study looking at the transition between KS2 and KS3, before moving onto some key principles for curriculum design and assessment.

TRANSITION FROM KS2 TO KS3

Rachel Cliffe, Head of History at a school in Leeds, @MrsRCliffe

Challenges

KS3 may be one of the first times your students have experienced history as a discrete subject, encountered historical terminology or been asked to complete a history assessment. However, you may have some students who have had a rich experience of historical vocabulary and grasp the second-order concepts of cause, consequence and even significance. The complexity of having students from several feeder primary schools with varying experience of history as a subject has an impact on KS3 curriculum planning, and if the transition is not smooth, it can impact a student's enjoyment of the subject.

Gathering information

I gathered information about the KS2 history curriculum as part of a curriculum transition project. The steps I took to gather information are given below. I hope that they will be a help to you if you also want to think more about the KS2 to KS3 transition.

The starting point for my project was to get to grips with the KS2 National Curriculum. It outlines the skills students should develop and the content that should be covered. Skills at KS2 include establishing clear narratives within and across topics and regularly addressing historically valid questions. The content includes one post-1066 study, a wider world study and pre-1066 units. Yet it does not state that history should be taught as a discrete subject, and primary schools can choose to teach the content as part of a wider theme or study. Therefore, for example, students may answer historical questions, but the focus may be on literacy skills.

We contacted our feeder primary schools via our transition lead. I chose to send a Google Form to the transition staff at the feeder primary schools to ascertain how history is taught, the specific topics taught and whether history was assessed. The use of the Google Form was to make it quick and easy through multiple-choice questions, and it did the analysis of the results for me! If you do not have the links to feeder primary schools, contact your transition lead member of staff or use the school webpages to look at the history curriculum for the main feeder primary schools.

To build a positive relationship with the feeder primary schools, I also created a History Primary Guide to support the development of historical skills in each primary and to open up contact with the history leads. The guide included definitions of second-order concepts and prompts to help primary teachers develop historically valid questions in their curriculum. The guide was created in collaboration with one of the feeder primary schools and their history lead, and emailed out along with the Google Form.

Findings

There were 15 responses from feeder primary schools and the findings were interesting. There was a real mixture of history being a discrete subject or part of a topic-based curriculum. In most feeder schools, history was not formally assessed or was assessed against skills statements like 'I can describe the Blitz in World War Two'. The schools tended to cover two or three history topics in each year of KS2.

Impact on KS3 curriculum

After reviewing the KS2 history curricula for the six main feeder primary schools, we found that chronology needed to be a key focus of our curriculum, due to the placement of topics taught. For example, one feeder school studies the slave trade and then the Egyptians in Year 5. Is there an understanding of the chronological gap between the two periods? The format of our KS3 curriculum is chronological, with the intent of building a secure chronological understanding. Furthermore, we found that every feeder primary school taught World War Two with a focus on the home front. We therefore adapted our World War Two unit to make it a global study. We still reference the home front within our enquiry, to allow students to recall KS2 knowledge, but the emphasis is on a comparison to other countries during World War Two, including India, occupied France and Singapore, rather than explicitly teaching the British home front. In our pre-1066 unit, we decided to develop a focus on retrieving and developing KS2 knowledge. We also added material on the importance of local history, as the local topic chosen varied between primary schools.

We used a professional development session to look at the KS2 National Curriculum, analyse the KS2 curriculum from our main feeder primary school and look at some 'deep dive'-style questions. We then outlined how we build upon and develop the KS2 topics and how this links to our intent. The department is now much more confident in explaining our curriculum intent and rationale.

The findings also affected our assessment. For most of our history students, the first Year 7 assessment would be their very first time answering historical questions for the purpose of their knowledge and skills being assessed. This led us to change the structure, question styles and scaffolding for all assessments across Year 7. Our first assessment now has a knowledge section with multiple-choice questions and then a consequence question to answer with scaffolded guidance and sentence starters, so students have an awareness of how much to write and what to write. The assessments across Year 7 also have timings included, so students spend an appropriate amount of time on each question. The scaffolding reduces as the year progresses, to build students' confidence with historical skills. Compared to our previous assessment styles, this is much more accessible and acknowledges students' lack of experience with history assessments.

A further consequence of the project has been building further links with history leads in the feeder primary schools. Since the project, I have had email exchanges regarding subject knowledge, sent out example Year 7 assessments and had a history lead visit the department for an afternoon to watch lessons. I also hope to have the opportunity to see KS2 history being taught and to look at historical writing in KS2.

Whilst this was a specific transition project, there are elements that you can consider in order to develop your own curriculum design and knowledge. For example, you might like to build your understanding of the KS2 National Curriculum, look at the webpages for feeder primary schools or consider your first Year 7 assessment and the accessibility. Equally, this may inspire you to contact the feeder primary schools and launch your own project!

Evaluating your content selection

When reflecting upon your whole history curriculum provision from KS3 to KS5, consider the following questions:

- Is it broad and balanced?
- Is there a balance of cultural, economic, political, social and military history?
- Which individuals or groups are seen or heard the most?
- Is there a balance of second-order concepts? (See below.)

- Are students able to see themselves reflected in the curriculum?

- Is there a range of time periods?

- Is there a balance of periods and chronological scope?

A well-designed curriculum typically has a clear and well-thought-out explanation for why certain content is emphasised. This explanation should take into account how the content facilitates future learning, all the while maintaining a balance between curriculum breadth and coherence.

Second-order concepts

Second-order concepts shape the way we understand, organise and discuss knowledge. In history, second-order concepts include:

- causation

- evidence/sources

- interpretations

- change and continuity

- significance.

When building your long-term plan, consider how and when you will tackle second-order concepts across your curriculum, and their breadth and scope.

When we reviewed our KS3 curriculum to make it three years long (see Chapter 1), we considered our coverage of second-order concepts, and noticed that we had too many causation units and that change and continuity and significance were not embedded. Therefore, our Year 9 curriculum had to cater for this, and we included topics like the ones below.

- British Empire through time: This provides some excellent opportunities for similarity and difference by comparing experiences of colonisation between different places and periods.

- British civil rights: This unit asks how important people were in advancing their own rights.

Sequencing

Once you have matched second-order concepts with key content that you want to cover, spend some time arranging and repairing the order in which you will teach them.

For us, our KS3 and KS4 curriculum is mostly taught in chronological order, whereas our KS5 curriculum is sequenced in terms of progression of skills.

These are some example considerations when sequencing your curriculum:

- Are there any cross-curricular links to be considered?

- One thematic study is required at GCSE according to the Department for Education (DfE). Where should you place this thematic study? (Thematic studies often work well at the end of a course, as students tend to need a lot of contextual knowledge to be able to navigate effectively through various periods.)

- How will you build knowledge across the whole key stage? (If you are planning to teach about the Reformation, for example, it is helpful for students to have previously studied the role of the Church in medieval England.)

Reflecting demographics

It is important to review how much of your curriculum reflects the demographic of your student population. Weave diversity into the units you can, as well as weaving in local histories. Diversity in the curriculum is discussed in more detail in Chapter 3.

Using overarching questions

You might like to use an overarching question to help structure your curriculum. Elizabeth Carr discusses this approach in her case study.

USING OVERARCHING QUESTIONS IN HISTORY

Elizabeth Carr, Subject Lead for Humanities at Avanti Grange Secondary School, Bishop's Stortford, Hertfordshire

An overarching question is a single question to which we return over the course of the year. We ensure that students can begin to answer it within the first half term of the course in each year. This is important because it means that we can introduce the question at the start of the year, and students can quickly make sense of it and begin to answer it.

Almost every enquiry we study, and indeed every lesson, will have some connection to the overarching question (although some connections may be more tenuous than others). In theory, therefore, every lesson of the curriculum contributes a small piece of the jigsaw that students could use to answer it.

The overarching question does not replace enquiry questions in our curriculum. Each lesson sequence is governed by its own, tightly focused and carefully phrased enquiry question linked to a disciplinary concept. The overarching question is, necessarily, much more open.

We currently use these three overarching questions in our KS3 curriculum:

- Year 7: How were different places in the world connected before 1492?
- Year 8: How did revolutions transform the world after 1492?
- Year 9: For what should the twentieth century be remembered?

These questions, and the way we currently use them, were greatly influenced by the work of Tom Allen, whose Curricularium (2020) presentation prompted me to review and refine our use of overarching questions.

A benefit of the overarching question is the sense of direction and coherence it lends to our curriculum, for both students and teachers. Whilst thinking deeply about each of our enquiry questions, we also constantly reference the overarching question and draw out the links between our current topic of study and the bigger picture. It helps us to make links to previous topics, and it helps students to see the relevance of some of the less familiar topics in our curriculum in particular. They seem to find it reassuring to know that there is a plan!

The decisive benefit of using an overarching question is its value for assessment. Over the course of the curriculum, students build up a growing schema of substantive knowledge relevant to the overarching question. We use the question itself as a summative assessment question. Students can make an initial answer early on, perhaps around half term in October; by February, they can add to and develop that answer in the light of new knowledge and understanding they have acquired from recent topics, whilst continuing to draw on their knowledge from earlier in the year. At the end of the year, students know enough, and feel confident enough, to further extend and develop their answers to the question.

We can compare students' answers to the overarching question at different stages in the year to make inferences about their knowledge and the progress they have made. This provides one valuable tool in our assessment toolbox. We combine the outcomes from the overarching question with data from other types of assessment question, including students' answers to each enquiry question, multiple-choice questions and timeline questions, to inform our summative assessments.

We have found that some students continue to fall back on their earlier answers, writing again about the topics from the beginning of the year, with which they feel most comfortable. This is not necessarily a concern: it demonstrates their recall of what they learned earlier in the year, and that they recognise the value of remembering what they have learned. The overarching question has certainly helped to introduce spacing and retrieval into the curriculum, supporting students' long-term recall. We now use guidelines, such as a number of topics or geographical locations students should include, to nudge the less confident to go beyond their favoured topics.

We also began varying the question in assessment from Year 8 onwards. We asked questions that related to the overarching question, but narrowed it in particular ways or rephrased it. Our overarching question in Year 8 asks about the transformative effects of revolutions. As an assessment question, we asked students what they had learned about revolution as a concept. An alternative would be to retain the focus on change (transformation) in the question, but ask about a related concept from the curriculum, such as protest, rebellion, religion or empire. Students still draw on the same knowledge to answer these questions but have to think on their feet a little more to identify which knowledge is relevant and to tailor it to the question. This makes it a useful assessment of the flexibility of students' knowledge.

Shaping enquiry questions

Give each topic a shape through an enquiry question. Having an enquiry question in mind is important in curriculum planning. It helps to filter the knowledge we need to include in lessons, as well as work out the sequencing of knowledge. Chapter 4 explains how to create effective enquiry questions in more depth.

Once I have thought of an enquiry, I then write an essay. Each paragraph within my essay then becomes my lesson. If you cannot write an essay to the enquiry question you have created, then you need to rethink and devise a new one.

For example, our civil rights enquiry is: 'What did Black activism achieve for African-Americans?' I wrote an essay. From this essay, I structured my paragraphs into the following:

1. Problems African-Americans faced after emancipation.

2. The actions and impact of early activists, such as Fredrick Douglass, Booker T. Washington, Ida B. Wells-Barnett, William E. B. Du Bois (commonly known as W. E. B. Du Bois) and Marcus Garvey.

3. The actions and impact of the National Association for the Advancement of Colored People (NAACP).

4. The actions and impact of Martin Luther King.

5. The actions and impact of Malcolm X.

6. The actions and impact of the Black Panther Party.

7. Conclusion on what was achieved for African-Americans and who made the greatest contribution.

These paragraphs essentially became my lesson topics (see below).

Effective planning requires you to work backwards. Having this essay meant that I had the end product, and so it became easy to plan the earlier stages.

At KS3, we also use our enquiry questions as our assessment questions (see later sections in this chapter).

Lesson topics

Your lesson topics can come from writing an essay in answer to your enquiry. The process of writing an essay will help you to break the content down into lesson-sized chunks. Title every lesson with a smaller question that feeds into the overall enquiry. For example:

Enquiry: What did Black activism achieve for African-Americans?

Lesson 1: What problems did enslaved Africans face after emancipation?
Lesson 2: What did early activists achieve for African-Americans?
Lesson 3: What did the NAACP achieve for African-Americans?
Lesson 4: What did Martin Luther King achieve for African-Americans?
Lesson 5: What did Malcolm X achieve for African-Americans?
Lesson 6: What did the Black Panther Party achieve for African-Americans?
Lesson 7: Assessment

Vocabulary

Having decided on the different topics to cover in each lesson, spend some time identifying and noting key words for each lesson and unit. These are useful for improving student vocabulary and helping them get to grips with concepts they will be discussing in class. Tom Hopkins-Burke provides some great strategies for teaching vocabulary in his case study in Chapter 10.

Teacher knowledge

Once you have planned your framework of the topics and lessons you will be teaching, spend some time building your knowledge in historical scholarship surrounding the topics you will be teaching. Improving your teacher knowledge will help you to plan and teach lessons effectively. Reading and listening to podcasts can also provide quotes, interpretations, stories or other information to help enrich lessons and bring them to life. See Chapter 11 for more on developing your subject knowledge.

REFRESHING A CURRICULUM

Ammar Khan, Head of History in London, @MrKhan_history

As a department, we decided to refresh our A level course. Our teaching at the time consisted of the Stuarts, the Russian Revolution and civil rights in the USA. We read *Empireland* (2021) by Sathnam Sanghera and felt this was important to teach at A level. It complemented our focus on key substantive historical concepts. We decided a study of the British Empire from 1857–1965 would allow us to explore the concepts in greater depth. We considered the best option to be an OCR course, as it offered the most flexibility in selecting other topics. We also decided to teach Britain from 1930–1997. This was primarily to explore our chosen substantive historical concepts in a different context but also – together with the Empire paper – to provide students with a comprehensive understanding of British society today. Planning a new A level course takes a lot of time; our new topics would only be implemented two years later.

Once our end point of the curriculum was secure, we could then decide what to teach earlier in the curriculum with greater clarity. At GCSE level, Edexcel brought out a new course, 'Migrants in Britain', and there was unanimous agreement within the department that we should teach this. However, we decided not to teach it to our Year 10 cohort straight away, to allow us time to improve subject knowledge, plan and resource 'Migrants in Britain', as well as refine our KS3 teaching. That year, instead, students began their GCSE course with the Paper 3 option: 'Weimar and Nazi Germany, 1918–39', as the Year 11s also needed to learn this topic at that time.

Enthused and motivated by our key concepts, we then began developing the KS3 curriculum. This continues to be an area of ongoing growth. The history curriculum map is very different to what it used to be, and I anticipate continuing to refine our students' learning journey as time progresses. The curriculum has gone through multiple versions and adaptations, and this is a good thing, as it evidences that the department is in a state of continuous development. At KS3, we are not restricted by exam specifications and the National Curriculum is relatively flexible, so we have been able to focus on achieving our department aims and explore our overarching key concepts unimpeded. Together with the curriculum intent, specific aims for KS3 were established. They are:

- chronological sequencing
- year groups to focus on specific overarching concepts
- a broader geographical range
- a mix of breadth and depth topics
- connections to local history
- enquiry-based focus
- to be underpinned by disciplinary knowledge.

As a result, we felt that we had enough of the framework to start thinking hard about our history curriculum and its redesign. Topic choices were justified with reasoned criteria. We developed the curriculum during department meetings, which were rich in the discussion of history and the knowledge we want students to have.

Overall, the process of redesigning our history curriculum has been an incredibly rewarding experience. It has brought the history department together with a common purpose and we have genuinely enjoyed spending department hours thinking over the correct sequencing of topics throughout the curriculum. This can only be a good thing.

CURRICULUM DESIGN PRINCIPLES

Ashley Bartlett, Curriculum Leader of History and Lead Subject Tutor for History

1. The National Curriculum is NOT your enemy

When the current incarnation of the National Curriculum was published in 2012, much was written about it being 'British-centric', 'lacking diversity' and being 'narrow'. Indeed, these calls only intensified during the Black Lives Matter movement. As with anything in history, however, the above is one interpretation... You can choose to see the National Curriculum as a delightfully vague, three-page document. The *only* statutory content in the current KS3 history curriculum is the Holocaust; beyond that, as long as one is broad and balanced, then the world is your oyster... Embrace the freedoms of the National Curriculum and make it your own. The alternative is a centralised, dictated and multipage tome (I have been around long enough to remember those). So, do not blame the National Curriculum for a lack of diversity in a curriculum.

2. Ensure your curriculum represents twenty-first-century Britain

No curriculum should be 'diverse' for diversity's sake, but it should be representative of the community you serve. Students need to see themselves reflected in it, and if your cohort is exclusively White, then it is even more important that they recognise that Britain's history, and indeed the wider society today, is not. A history curriculum should be a reflection of the best that has been thought and said; some of this has been uttered by White men, Black women, members of the LGBTQIA+ community… all of whom should be not only be represented within our curriculum, but woven into it throughout.

3. Have a golden thread to bind it

Weaving a curriculum requires a 'golden thread' to bind it. You will choose yours. For me, it is local history. We serve a brilliantly diverse community. What combines us all is the fact that we have all ended up, through a variety of experiences, living and working in Leicester. Providing young people with a thread of local history that they can walk past, see and share with their families, and which unites us all, is key to binding the curriculum and the community together. We have worked closely with Historic England to be recognised as a 'Heritage School' and this has been hugely influential in developing and supporting this approach.

Assessment is an important area in education; it is needed to judge the success of any teaching and learning and inform the design and adaptation of plans for future learning. There are two types of assessment: summative and formative. Summative assessment focuses on what has been learned. Formative assessment focuses on what still needs to be learned. We will consider formative assessment in later chapters, in particular Chapter 7. Here we consider summative assessment and its part in curriculum design.

Summative assessment

Summative assessment is the final showcase of learning, typically at the end of a unit or enquiry. It brings together the thinking from a number of lessons. The aim of summative assessment is to assess student progress and to provide feedback for both student and teacher on how a unit or enquiry of lessons have gone.

It is important to know what progress looks like in history. For example, how will you be able to tell that students are getting better at understanding causation? Does this fit in with the assessment criteria that you are using to track?

Devise criteria for what progress looks like within each historical concept. The 'progression of concepts model document' (Figure 2.1) is a useful tool to help you do this. In your department, note down the various skills needed to be successful in understanding each historical concept and what students should be able to do at each stage of progression. This will also help you to plan for explicit teaching of the various skills at different points within the curriculum.

Creating a progression model will give your team a shared understanding of what progression in history looks like for students in your school from Year 7 to Year 13. Research

What progress looks like with...	Beginner	Developing	Expert/mastery
Sources	Understands the source in the context of the time period. Provides inferences.	Supports inferences with accurate knowledge. Selects accurate sources to supplement a historical narrative.	Evaluates the provenance of the source.
Significance			
Interpretations			
Causation			
Change and continuity			
Similarity and difference			

FIGURE 2.1: *Progression of concepts model*

by Lee and Ashby (2000) shows that students' progress in different concepts does not necessarily develop at the same rate, i.e. a student's ideas about sources may remain the same whilst their ideas about interpretations are changing rapidly. It is therefore helpful to be able to look at each concept individually.

Creating a progression model will also show you the range of ideas your students are likely to encounter, and the kind of changes you are likely to see as students' learning develops. The progression model can also help to inform your mark scheme.

Summative assessment at KS3

In September 2020, I became head of history and wanted to revamp KS3. One of the areas I wanted to improve was summative assessment. Our KS3 assessments used GCSE-style questions, which was problematic as it was reductive. GCSEs are meant to provide insight into a very specific domain over two years; therefore, they cannot be representative of all that school history has to offer. Furthermore, GCSE is a points-based system and translating that into a mark scheme for KS3 students is not fair, accurate or realistic. Consequently, we made changes. Figure 2.2 shows our new model.

As the table shows, our KS3 assessments typically have two parts: part 1 is a knowledge test and part 2 is an extended answer to the enquiry question. Students plan for this enquiry throughout the series of lessons within the plenary segment at the end of each lesson. This is so that students can connect together lessons along the way and not lose focus from the enquiry question. This ensures that the assessment is fair and equitable for all students.

The next steps of assessment improvement would be for students to answer the overarching enquiry question at the

	PART 1 – Knowledge test	PART 2 – Extended writing
Types of assessment tasks	• Quiz • Fill in the gaps • 'Complete the timeline from memory' task	• Essay answering the enquiry question • Write a historical narrative account using sources to construct your answer • Extended essay question on a source, e.g. 'How helpful is source X for a historian researching Y' (enquiry question) or give students five various sources and ask them to select two sources that would be the most helpful for a historian investigating Y • Extended essay question on an interpretation

FIGURE 2.2: *KS3 assessment model*

end of two or three enquiries so that they are connecting knowledge gained from enquiries together.

Preparing students for summative assessment

It is helpful to give students time to prepare before a summative assessment. I find the following two strategies particularly useful.

Creating a class plan

Before an assessment, I tend to plan collaboratively with the class using various modelling techniques (outlined in Chapter 6) to go through a question similar to their assessment question. This exposes students to excellence in terms of procedural and conceptual knowledge.

Discussion

Discussion allows students to talk to each other before writing up their assessments, which helps them to assess the potency of their arguments. I find this method useful when teaching A level students how to sustain their argument. Giving discussion time beforehand allows students to test their arguments and think more deeply about the evidence they need to include.

Summary

- Consider your students' KS2 history learning, particularly when designing your KS3 curriculum.

- Ensure your curriculum is broad and balanced.

- Make sure that there is balanced coverage of second-order concepts.

- Work out how you would like to sequence your curriculum (for example, chronologically, by progression of skills or linked to other subjects).

- Ensure your curriculum reflects the demographic of your student population.

- Use overarching questions to structure your curriculum.

- Use enquiry questioning to break the unit topics down into individual lesson topics.

- Identify key words for units and lessons.

- Consider teacher knowledge of topics, including whether teacher knowledge needs to be developed.

- When looking at summative assessment, construct models of progression to assess key historical concepts (e.g. sources, significance, interpretations, etc.).

- Consider the best format for summative assessment at KS3.

- Prepare students well for assessments, especially by using an enquiry question for a topic that students refer to in every lesson.

3

A diverse curriculum

In this chapter we will focus on creating a diverse curriculum. It is crucial that our curricula engage students and provide intellectual challenge to students from all backgrounds. Diversity overlaps with issues of inclusion in many ways, and there is plenty of data showing how a student's background has a profound impact on their achievements in school. The reasons for this are complex, but the content of the curriculum is one factor.

Diversifying content

History is naturally diverse, as it includes the history of many different social groups. It follows, then, that one way to address the question of diversity is to teach a diverse range of content. To do this, we need to diversify our own subject knowledge. Flora Wilson wrote on this in her article, 'How my interest in what I don't teach informed my teaching and enriched my students' learning' (Wilson, 2012).

Diversifying second-order concepts

It is important to embed diversity throughout your curriculum. Teaching a diverse range of content is important, but Bradshaw

(2009) asserts that diversity is more than this. He argues that diversity needs to be considered a second-order concept involving processes of analysis and judgement. Pearson (2012) also links diversity to second-order concepts such as significance. She says that the danger of simply introducing additional content is that a transmission model of teaching is adopted, which lacks challenge. Instead, an approach is needed that combines different content with a rigorous conceptual challenge. This is likely to be engaging for students and provides a means for developing more sophisticated historical reasoning.

For example, Tom Sims (@Tommole) produced an excellent four-lesson introductory enquiry called 'How do we become historians?' using David Olusoga's book *Black and British* (2020) to introduce historical skills (see Chapter 4). These skills include chronology, sources, interpretations and writing like a historian. Sometimes our curricula can implicitly suggest that Westernisation or White history is the centre of history, or that history starts with White people and they are the main characters. However, Tom's enquiry does not start with White history. This is a great way to show the importance of previously hidden stories. Furthermore, rather than learning concepts in the abstract, his enquiry provides students with the context they need in order to develop their understanding.

How to set about diversifying your curriculum

Over the next few pages, I give some of my top tips on ways to diversify your curriculum. Many of my examples look at Black British history, as this has been a particular interest of mine, but the principles can and should be applied across different people groups.

1. Weave, blend and integrate diverse stories

When teaching the more traditional topics like the World Wars, the Industrial Revolution, medieval England, the Romans and the Tudors, etc., we should weave in diverse stories. For example, we make sure that photographs we show include Black and Brown faces as well as White. The British Library and the Imperial War Museum have great resources you can use.

When teaching the Year 7 introductory unit 'What is history?', we include non-Western sources, such as Ghanaian kente cloth, proverbs and oral histories from the African continent. This shows that historical sources come in various formats.

When teaching the civil rights movement in the USA, we do a comparative study with the UK civil rights movement, and ask questions such as: 'To what extent was the UK civil rights movement influenced by the US civil rights movement?' or 'Why did the British government introduce the Race Relations Act in 1968?'

2. Look at your local and regional stories

Make connections to your school's local area, as this gives meaning to students.

If your school is based outside of London, local history can help your students to see that diverse stories are not just from London. If you teach in London, it is still important to look at diverse stories from rural areas. The 'Colonial Countryside' project by Dr Corinne Fowler, in connection with the University of Leicester and the National Trust, is a great resource if you are teaching Black British history. She explores the countryside's links to empire and slavery.

One way you can include diverse stories in your local histories is by students completing 'meanwhile nearby' worksheets for homework. Resources for researching your local area include:

- county records office
- local archives
- Historic England
- British Library
- local parish records.

3. Rigorous enquiry questions

Presenting diverse figures and stories in British history, particularly pre-1945, can sometimes arouse disbelief or even anger. This can be seen in the debate surrounding a BBC Teach video about Roman Britain that featured a fictional Roman family made up of a Black father, White mother and children of mixed heritage.

Creating enquiries centred on disciplinary thinking can help students to focus on the evidence rather than assumptions. Hannah Cusworth has created enquiry questions such as 'How did Miranda Kauffmann uncover the lives of Black Tudors?' (2021). Hannah's enquiry inspired me to create a lesson with the title: 'How have historians and archaeologists uncovered the existence of Black people in Roman and medieval Britain?' Through this lesson, students learned about methods that archaeologists use to uncover the Black presence, such as craniometrics, chemical analysis and bone measurement.

4. Sources

It is important that sources feature in our teaching as much as possible. Sources provide an authentic window into people's experiences and give agency to them. Looking back at my old lessons, I am ashamed to say that sources were only featured in 'source' enquiries or lessons looking at GCSE papers assessing source skills. It was not something that featured in all our lessons. My department and I are still working on including more sources. As we have created lessons for migration at KS4, we have ensured that sources feature in every lesson, despite half the paper not assessing source skills. We do this by introducing a source before distilling the content. Therefore, before students learn about the reasons why Africans came to England in the early modern period, they have to work out the reasons from the source. Not only are they exercising their inference skills, but they are also thinking hard and recognising the value of sources as a source of information rather than as simply a way of assessing utility or reliability. We get our sources from places such as the migration module textbooks, the Our Migration Story website, the National Archives and the Black Cultural Archives.

When including pictures or photo sources, consider colourism as well. This was highlighted to me through Hannah Cusworth's article 'Putting Black into the Union Jack: weaving Black history into the Year 7 to 9 curriculum' (2021). When incorporating photos from the past make sure that, in addition to including light-skinned individuals or those with mixed heritage, such as Walter Tull, Mary Seacole or Dido Belle, include the impact of dark-skinned figures. Do not just include darker-skinned figures when teaching about slavery.

5. Individual stories

Stories help to provide a richer understanding of the imagined past. They are the micro perspective that help students' understanding of the macro perspective. Not every story can be taught but select the story or stories that can give your students a panoramic view into typical experiences for different people groups. Just as with using more sources, using stories can provide authenticity in what we teach. Most importantly, stories help students to connect to the past on a human level. Stories also have cognitive benefits. Daniel Willingham has shown that using stories helps to aid memory. According to Willingham (2004), stories are 'psychologically privileged' because they are more interesting, easier to understand and easier to remember.

Here are some examples of lesson titles centred on stories of individuals:

- What does the story of Cornelia Sorabji reveal about Asian migration in Britain in 1700–1900?

- What does Kelso Cochrane's story reveal about race relations?

- What does Fanny Eaton's story reveal about Victorian ideas about race?

6. Consider how to approach language

If a child used certain language in the playground, we would sanction them. Therefore, to use the same language in a lesson because it is in a source is contentious. Black students in my school have expressed their concerns with the N-word being used in their English lessons when reading *Of Mice and Men*. They did not want this word to gain any legitimacy by being used in a classroom. I think that students' feelings on this issue should be respected.

I, personally, do not feel comfortable with avoiding words without comment or discussion. Surely, it would leave our students ignorant if we did this. Hannah Cusworth recommends teaching students about a word's etymology, context and how it is used and heard today, and establishing any rules on its usage in and outside of the classroom (Cusworth, 2021). Discuss as a department how to approach language and become aware of how some students may react to particular words being used in your classroom.

7. Make classrooms 'safe spaces'

There are aspects of history that can be uncomfortable or sensitive or evoke many emotions. After Joanne Maraschin (@JoanneMaraschin) posted on my blog, I have tried to use my classroom as a safe space: 'a safe space for my Black students to raise issues without fear of being labelled "militant" or "angry"… a space where my White students could address their fears, prejudices and misconceptions without fear of being labelled "racist" or "ignorant"' (Maraschin, 2020). As Maraschin writes, we can also 'extend our outcomes to include *values* like empathy, understanding, appreciation, and listening – then we will soon realise the depth of learning in a history classroom is far greater [and will serve students beyond the classroom]' (Maraschin, 2020).

Case studies

The case studies that follow offer a variety of contexts and approaches to diversifying your curriculum.

QUESTIONS TO ASK YOURSELF AND HOW TO RESOURCE YOUR CURRICULUM

Natasha De Stefano Honey, Second in Charge of History and Politics in a state school in South London and Early Career Teacher (ECT) induction mentor, @GreenteaMiss

Questions we ask ourselves

I devised a set of questions that we could keep returning to at the end of the year and again at the start of the next as a reminder, and to ensure a clear focus on our vision.

1. **Can we ensure the pasts of *all students* we teach are represented in our curriculum?** I looked at the cohort of students in our school to ensure that their histories were being reflected. I considered genders, nationalities and social classes. This is something that will continue to change and will be different for every school.

2. **Are the pasts of the people of *modern Britain* represented in our curriculum across the key stages?** The history of migration is a key feature of our GCSE breadth study unit and runs through our KS3 course. The narrative of migration and empire runs through the key stages. Fights for change within Britain also feature heavily in our units because of this question.

3. **When we use visuals, do they show the *diversity of people* who were in the past and respect their dignity?** The impact of a visual source is immediate: students are affected as soon as they are exposed to pictures and clips. Therefore, staff ask themselves this question whenever they are selecting sources for their lessons. We ensure that visuals are not used to shock or 'hook' and should be respectful of the trauma various groups have faced (hook pictures have a place elsewhere in topics).

4. **Can we use a *diverse range of sources*? In addition, when we include the work of historians and other 'authority' figures, do we draw on work from a diverse and representative range of people?** Students need to see themselves in what we teach, not simply as the oppressed or the victor, but through the range

of historians we use. In time, this will create a more diverse group of historians to draw upon in lessons. The Royal Historical Society report of October 2018 stated that as of 2018, of all history academic staff, 93.7 per cent were White and 6.3 per cent were Black and minority ethnic, of whom just 0.5 per cent were Black (Atkinson et al., 2018). As history teachers, we should be letting our young people know that there is space for them in historical academia through our selection of sources.

5. **Will students know that Black people and people of colour have lived in Britain since very ancient times? Can we start this knowledge journey from Year 7?** From Year 7, our students know about Septimius Severus and are ready to defend Mary Beard after the Twitter storm of 2017 in their Roman unit. In our British-focused topics, they are aware, and we need to continue to make them know, that people of colour have always been part of Britain's history. For example, when studying the Chartists, William Cuffay and his work with trade unions is part of the story. Just having Black people feature in a unit on the transatlantic slave trade is problematic, and only celebrating Black history for Black History Month is tokenistic. As a department, we do not want to do either, as it is unfair to the students we are teaching.

6. **Will students be aware that 50 per cent of people in the past were women? Can we always tell students what women were doing?** As a child (and as an adult audience member at many CPD courses and academic lectures), I have always asked: 'What were women doing?' Women still do not feature in many of the GCSE and A level topics, and as teachers we find ourselves shoehorning in stories for representation. In all our units, we need to be prepared with an answer,

but equally women need a large enough percentage of the curriculum. When we are studying Walter Tull during our World War One unit, it leads into women's football before and during the period, and the story of Lily Parr and her contemporaries. When we are studying Alan Turing, our students are aware of the many women at Bletchley Park who were code-breaking, as well as the women involved in espionage. Every one of our KS3 units features women.

7. **Will students understand that the story of Black people and people of colour is not just one of people as victims of White oppression? Can we celebrate achievement throughout KS3?** We wanted to celebrate Black history and we wanted that celebration to be across the years. Black history cannot start with the transatlantic slave trade; there needs to be a celebration of the achievements Black people have made. So, for example, our Year 7s see Black people across the Roman Empire and through their Tudor topic, and in Year 8 they celebrate and learn about great African civilisations and, post the transatlantic slave trade, Black abolitionists and then civil rights leaders in both the USA and Britain, as well as our other topics.

8. **Can we get students to understand the class struggle?** Many of our students are from working-class backgrounds and it is important for our school that our students see that. In topics such as the Chartists and suffragette movements, we ensure that students see the working class creating change. Equally, in other units across the key stages, class is a feature; we have steered away from teaching a mainly upper-class narrative.

9. **How can we ensure students understand that groups such as Jewish people and Roma and Sinti people have a long history that is not just one of**

suspicion and oppression? As with the transatlantic slave trade and Black history, students must not be exposed to Jewish and Roma and Sinti history in the Holocaust only. Students need to know of successes, and a history that pre-exists the Nazis. Therefore, in our curriculum, we teach about thriving Jewish, Roma and Sinti communities. We also acknowledge that the Holocaust wiped out complete families and communities, some of which were not rebuilt after the war. The discrimination faced by these groups is a discussion point in lessons.

10. **Will students understand that that there have always been less visible groups, such as LGBTQIA+ people and people with disabilities, in society?** When studying groups that have been marginalised, it is important that their story is also seen, and that they too are celebrated. For example, in our Holocaust unit, we view Willem Arondéus's story as part of the resistance to the Nazis. In our suffragette topic, we include Rosa May Billinghurst (a member of the Women's Social and Political Union) so students know that those with disabilities have fought for change too. More and more resources are being produced to help teach disability within history fairly, but we should acknowledge hidden disabilities too. As a teacher who has attention deficit hyperactivity disorder (ADHD), dyslexia and dyspraxia, I know I need to research more stories.

Resourcing schemes of work – practical tips and tricks

- **Use university outreach programmes – for all key stages.** Universities are often keen to work with schools; many will send their lecturers to work with your students on projects. In my previous school, I ran the Milward Society and invited lecturers in every half term to speak about a wide range of topics. In my current school, a World War One project is run with a historian annually. Oxbridge and many Russell Group universities have outreach programmes and want to provide sessions for our students.

- **Be a 'magpie' and collect stories and ideas – you do not have to use them all at once.** Watch and read the news; stories are always emerging that you can use in your classroom. There are also many television programmes or podcasts with social history we can use, such as the BBC's *A House Through Time* presented by David Olusoga.

- **Visit museums.** Many museums are happy to help you. I have been to the People's Museum in Manchester to develop the visibility of disabled people within our curriculum. The Army Museum have visited our school on multiple occasions, with a visiting exhibit and mini lecture series for India's First War of Independence in our A level unit. The Migration Museum is also excellent and has online resources.

- **Realise your department is not an island.** It is not solely the job of the history team to ensure tokenism is avoided and your students have a range of diverse and inclusive histories and resources in lessons. Work together with departments across the school.

- **Use social media.** My favourite Instagram account is @thehistorycorridor – I may be Shalina Patel's biggest fan! I have gained so much knowledge from her account alone. X (formerly Twitter) is also fantastic for teachers: there are so many people to follow. I cannot include everyone here, but some fantastic accounts for inclusive history, and my favourites to magpie from, are: @missfolorunsho; @tenigogo_; @katieamery;

@misscarter89;   @justice2History;   @SashaL_Smith; @Lamb_heart_tea.

- **Do not reinvent the wheel – buy resources, if your budget allows.** Not every teacher loves making resources and/or has enough time to do so. Some of the more recent textbooks being released, as well as stand-alone online resources, are making steps to be far more inclusive than textbooks have ever been before. *40 Ways to Diversify the History Curriculum* by Elena Stevens (2022) is a practical guide with many lessons you can use directly in your department.
- **Explore free websites.** BBC Bitesize is excellent and they have many talented teachers developing diversity across their resources. The Black Curriculum website is outstanding and has free training for teachers, as well as many resources, as does the USI (Understanding Slavery Initiative). The National Archives have developed many free and inclusive resources for teachers too. Abdul Mohamud and Robin Whitburn's website and social media account @Justice2History are thought-provoking and helpful when updating your curriculum to be more inclusive.

It is important to remember that no school is the 'finished product' when it comes to teaching an inclusive history, and nor should they be. As history teachers, we should always be reviewing what we teach and making sure it is the best it can be for our students. Our students need a variety of histories, historians and sources in order for an inclusive history to be taught. I am very excited about the changes happening in the teaching of history and look forward to continually developing lessons with my department.

INTRODUCING A MORE DIVERSE HISTORY CURRICULUM TO A RELATIVELY MONO-CULTURAL COMMUNITY

Dr Simon Henderson, Deputy Headteacher and Head of Sixth Form at a rural school in County Durham

Diversity in the curriculum is important in the classroom and in the community to shape inclusive and nuanced understanding. I have spent a lot of my teaching career designing and delivering lessons and schemes of learning focused on providing a more nuanced narrative that seeks to expose students to different perspectives, voices and cultures. As a specialist in civil rights history and the Black freedom struggle, I have focused a lot on using stories from this element of the past to make wider points about inclusivity, freedom and justice.

More recently, my focus has been on redesigning the way that the curriculum engages with traditional topics highlighted on the history National Curriculum – for example, looking at the abolition of slavery in a way that takes the story back to the cultural and material wealth of African kingdoms pre-colonisation and explores the story of abolition beyond the standard Wilberforce narrative. My work on the *Black British History KS3 Teacher Resource Pack* (Folorunsho et al., 2022) focused on showing how Black people have shaped British life and been impacted by that experience. One of the key themes that runs throughout our KS3 curriculum is the construction of racial identity.

Over the course of 20-plus years working in the same school, there has been a small increase in the number of non-White faces in the classroom. Feedback from these students is that they appreciate seeing themselves more in the curriculum they follow. The impact the curriculum has had on the White students that dominate the cohort is also important. One of the most significant aspects of teaching a more diverse curriculum is confronting stereotypical and prejudiced ideas and discussing them in the classroom. One of the sections of the scheme of learning we follow on Black British history in the twentieth century looks at the role of Enoch Powell and the immigration debate of the 1960s and beyond. The lessons do not shy away from engaging directly with Powell's 'rivers of blood' speech and the government policy that tacitly supported the restriction of immigration from areas of the Commonwealth with majority Black populations.

Looking at prejudice, as well as views that speak against it, is central to understanding why the prejudice exists, where it comes from and how context shapes it. This can lead to difficult conversations (sometimes with parents who oppose some of the political aims of the Black Lives Matter movement, for example) and to challenges in the classroom, but it most often leads to empathy and an appreciation of seeing events through a lens beyond personal knowledge. One of the key skills of being an effective historian is, after all, this very disposition. White students cannot inhabit the same lived experience as their Black poors, but they can empathise and understand. As a result, the reception of a more inclusive and diverse curriculum has been overwhelmingly positive. As one student said after a lesson on the Notting Hill Carnival as a symbol of resistance to the racism that many immigrants faced: 'We have never learned about this before, but we really need to.'

DIVERSIFYING OUR KS3 CURRICULUM IN STAGES

Sian Ayling, Head of History in Kent, @MsAylingHist

You cannot do everything at once. As much as you would love to have a broad and inclusive curriculum throughout KS3 and KS4, taking on such a big task would either burn you out or water down the impacts you wanted to achieve.

It will also probably get harder before it gets easier. Break down and create a plan as to what steps you will take first, what needs to happen as soon as possible and what can wait for when you have more time. I would like to thank the Historical Association's Subject Leader Development Programme for helping me to understand this.

I soon came to realise that I could not change the whole of KS3 at once, so I took a two-fold approach. The curriculum for Year 7 would be completely new and follow the department's vision of each student feeling 'seen' and represented in the curriculum (see Figure 3.1). However, it would not be sustainable to do this for Years 8 and 9 at the same time. Therefore, my second approach was to include diverse histories throughout the remaining Year 8 and 9 curriculum. I placed them where they could have the largest impact and build greater meaning for students. For example, I added Empire soldiers into the teaching of who fought in World War One and Two (see Figure 3.2 for the proposed Year 8 and 9 future curriculum).

Developing subject knowledge

The aspect that can be most daunting when forming a diverse curriculum is confronting the sheer amount of

	Previous Year 7 curriculum	Updated Year 7 curriculum
Cycle A	How did William change England?	Who lived in Anglo-Saxon England?
		Did the Normans bring a 'truckload of trouble' to England? (Schama, 2000)
Cycle B	What was life like in medieval England?	What mattered to people in medieval England?
	What changes did medieval England experience?	Who held power in medieval England?
Cycle C	What did the Tudors do for Britain?	What travelled the Silk Roads?
		What made Abbasid Baghdad remarkable?
		What can Mansa Musa reveal about medieval Africa?
		How similar were transatlantic empires? (The Incas) / What can La Doncella reveal about the Incan Empire?
Cycle D	How was the world turned upside down in the sixteenth century?	How unlikely was a Tudor dynasty?
		Who lived in Tudor England?
		Did the Reformation cause more problems than it solved?

FIGURE 3.1: *Previous and updated Year 7 history curriculum*

	Year 8	Year 9
Cycle A	Why did Britain want an empire?	How should the Holocaust be remembered?
	How similar were experiences of colonisation?	Who resisted the Holocaust?
Cycle B	What was the transatlantic trade?	Why is there conflict in the Middle East? How far have other conflicts shaped the twentieth-century world? (Apartheid focus)
	How was the transatlantic trade resisted?	
Cycle C	Was the Industrial Revolution 'Liberty's Dawn'?	How similar was the process of decolonisation across the British Empire? (Ireland, Ghana, Jamaica, Nigeria, India)
	How close was Britain to a true democracy by 1900?	How similar was the process of decolonisation across empires?
Cycle D	What caused the Great War?	How has Britain changed throughout the twentieth century?
	Who fought in the Great War?	
	How did the Great War change Britain?	

FIGURE 3.2: *Proposed updated Year 8 and Year 9 curriculum*

history that you do not know. Be willing to share this load with the department if they are up for it. Work together to identify those quirky stories and the shared knowledge needed to feel comfortable to teach new histories. I sought to read, watch and listen to podcasts about the histories that were going into the new history curriculum. I followed the plan I previously created (Figure 3.1) and thought about what was urgent and what I could devote more time to later. I used resources from the Historical Association and the BeBold History Network, and attended CPD on African kingdoms and many other aspects.

Summary

- Be aware of the diversity of students in your school and ensure you design an inclusive curriculum in which all students can see themselves reflected.

- Consider ways to diversify your content and second-order concepts.

- Diversifying your curriculum takes time and requires revisiting regularly.

- Research and develop your own knowledge.

- Draw on the experiences of other teachers and schools who have spent time diversifying their curricula, such as those in the case studies included in this chapter.

4

Framing historical enquiries

Enquiry is fundamental to the study of history. The word 'historia' itself means 'enquiry'. In history teaching, the principle of structuring students' learning around a series of questions or enquiries that drives each unit of work is an effective way of teaching and learning. Enquiry questions give shape and coherence to the knowledge we teach. This chapter explores the benefits, features and uses of enquiry questions, as well as how to write and assess them.

Benefits of enquiry questions

Ian Dawson (ThinkingHistory.co.uk) suggests that enquiry can provide a model for students to develop independent learning skills, if the enquiry process is clearly described and explained.

Enquiry is, in effect, a form of problem-solving needed for the twenty-first-century global world. Historical enquiry develops students' ability to:

- effectively problem-solve
- conduct independent and team-driven research
- identify relevant evidence

- evaluate the reliability of the evidence
- move from tentative to firm conclusions on the basis of evidence
- confidently reach a judgement, balancing the arguments for and against
- become active constructors of meaning.

Crafting an enquiry question

Michael Riley (2008) suggests three ingredients for constructing a good enquiry question. It should:

- capture your students' imaginations
- foreground a particular aspect of historical thinking
- lead to an activity that allows students to answer the question.

Kyle Graham (2023, p. 130) adds to the checklist by posing the following questions:

- Is your enquiry question relevant to the full unit of work?
- Is it based explicitly on disciplinary knowledge?
- Is it an open-ended question that allows for challenge and a wide range of knowledge?
- Is it based in scholarship?

All of the questions in the checklists above need to be addressed simultaneously.

Here are some example enquiries that bear these considerations in mind:

- How far did the Normans bring a 'truckload of trouble' from 1066? (From Sian Ayling, see her case study in Chapter 3)

- What did African-American activism achieve for their rights from 1865–1970?

- Was the Industrial Revolution 'Liberty's Dawn'? (Griffin, 2013)

- What were the experiences of Empire soldiers on the Western Front?

- What did 'colonisation' mean to different countries in the British Empire?

- Who was to blame for the Cold War?

- How 'enlightened' were the American, French and Haitian revolutions?

- 'How did Miranda Kauffman uncover the lives of Black Tudors?' (Cusworth, 2021)

- How can we explain the English Civil War?

- What helped the struggle for equal rights in Britain after 1960?

These types of questions ensure that the enquiry spans the full length of a topic, and that there is enough scope for students to bring a wide range of knowledge into their answer. In essence, the enquiry question underpins the entire unit (see Chapter 2).

Enquiry questions help us to cover the disciplinary dimensions of history listed in the 2014 National Curriculum

(DfE, 2013). For example, if an enquiry question is framed with reference to the extent of change within a particular period, it builds understanding of change. If an enquiry question deals with the causes of an extraordinary event, then it helps students to understand causation. These sorts of questions teach students how to tackle different kinds of disciplinary questions. Enquiry questions demonstrate the need for detailed substantive knowledge to be able to reach a well-reasoned and substantiated answer. The enquiry question is also a planning device for teachers, enabling them to structure coherent sequences of lessons, building knowledge systematically within well-organised frameworks (see more on this in Chapter 2).

Involving students in writing enquiry questions

Sally Burnham (2007) was frustrated that her A level students were unable to frame good historical questions for their coursework. Recognising that this was an important skill for historians, and one that she ought to be developing throughout students' history education, she decided to allow her Year 7s to join her in planning enquiry questions that would structure their scheme of work on Islamic civilisations.

Her first step was to help the students distinguish between big and little questions related to their previous study of medieval history. She then offered several kinds of stimulus in turn – maps, a role play, written descriptions and visual sources – to generate questions for the new topic. This is a great idea as it mirrors the process historians use to embark on their research. The students then worked in groups, not only to plan and sequence the questions that they judged most interesting and worthwhile, but also to ensure that they addressed the key aspects of the topic they would cover.

Burnham developed the final scheme of work, drawing on planning grids produced by the students working in groups, with each of them able to identify where their questions had been used. Burnham was convinced of the value of the strategy and so repeated it in Year 8, building on the process by inviting the students to evaluate and, if necessary, adjust the questions in light of the available resources.

Pitfalls to avoid in devising enquiry questions

I am guilty of creating questions in the past that have required students to use the present lens to make judgements, such as: 'Was King John bad or good?' These questions encourage students to draw on their modern understanding of leadership, rather than helping them to understand differences in the ideas and values of people in past societies. It also incorrectly encourages students to draw upon their own values and attitudes without understanding the context, values and attitudes of people at different times in the past, which leaves students with misconceptions. There is also less focus on how historians learn about and communicate ideas about past societies.

It is no good capturing your students' interest and imagination and tempting them with an intriguing mystery if the question they are seeking to answer is not rigorous and clearly rooted in historical concepts, process and scholarship. Nor is it enough to provide a tantalising hook, a real puzzle to solve, if students cannot develop a well-substantiated answer to the question. Good questions work effectively for students working at very different levels of attainment, allowing scope for nuanced and developed argument.

Furthermore, for an enquiry to produce successful outcomes for students, it is important that the enquiry question is revisited at the start or end of every lesson. For example, our common plenary task at KS3 is to get students to apply what they have learned so far to the enquiry question.

Finally, always ensure that:

- you identify a range of knowledge that would allow students to answer the enquiry question – so that you identify the most crucial knowledge for pupils to learn and for you to emphasise when teaching

- the questions you devise are grounded in the traditions of historical enquiry

- you avoid creating questions that strongly suggest there is a particular 'right' answer to complex historical questions

- you avoid framing questions in a way that might encourage pupils to take a particular moral or political position on contested issues.

PREPARING AND ASSESSING YOUR ENQUIRY QUESTION

Tom Sims, Head of History and Politics at a school in Mansfield

Key features of an enquiry question

During my teacher training, a wise head once told me that if I wanted to see a good lesson structure, I should watch *News at Ten*: a brief outline to start, swiftly followed by key information delivered in a crisp, clear and deliberate manner, which is then reviewed part-way through. Documentaries could perhaps provide an equivalent analogy for a historical enquiry.

Like news bulletins, documentaries have an important story to tell, but they do so in long-form, vividly and with great clarity. They often have an abundance of source material to work with, and must therefore be selective: identifying, choosing and sequencing the information in a way that is clearest. Crucially, they also bring the subject matter to life, prompting a personal response from the audience.

A key feature of an excellent enquiry is that it is rooted in what you want students to develop, be it particular elements of content you have identified as being of value, second-order concepts or historiographical techniques.

Another important element to consider is how the enquiry fits within your broader department priorities and your wider professional responsibilities as a teacher of history. Many history departments will currently be grappling with the challenge of how to introduce more reading and scholarship into their curriculum, in a way that avoids the sense that it has been 'bolted on' to existing resources. An excellent way to accomplish this is to build enquiries around books. For example, I developed a historical skills enquiry based around David Olusoga's book *Black and British* (2020), mentioned in Chapter 3 of this book. This approach provides many opportunities for incorporating reading activities. Additionally, books and scholarship will often reflect contemporary perspectives and debates around the topic focus, which is useful when determining an enquiry focus.

The enquiry question should represent the initial stage of your thinking, and should always be at the forefront of your mind when designing and resourcing your lessons. Identify the question first, and then select the content that best tells that story.

Preparing your enquiry

Once the conception of the enquiry has begun to take shape, the preparation stage will begin. Do not rush it. Many of my most successful enquiries have been months in the making, and at times it may look as if little progress is being made at all. Decide on your question, create a rough outline of your enquiry and then go hunting for treasure. For example, my department's Year 8 study of the British Empire is framed around two enquiry questions: 'Why is the British Empire "the prism through which the rest of the world views Britain"?' (Sanghera, 2021) and 'How should we remember the British Empire?' These enquiries were inspired by an online talk with the author Sathnam Sanghera, facilitated by the History Teacher Book Club, in which he discussed his book *Empireland* and its application in the classroom. By the end of the talk, I had sketched out the two enquiries and a lesson-by-lesson outline.

If I had planned and resourced the whole enquiry over the next fortnight, it would not have been anywhere near as impactful as it ended up being, nearly a year down the line. Over that time, I immersed myself in books, websites and archive material. I familiarised myself with contemporary debates around the topic. Non-fiction books, related fiction, textbooks, documentaries and podcasts were all invaluable sources of information that presented the material in a different way. The more I consumed, the more I was able to identify pertinent sources of information. Every time I found something useful, I filed it away. Most of this never ended up in the final version of the enquiry, but not a single moment of it was wasted.

The more time you can spend preparing your enquiry, the quicker it should be to construct. In my experience, at this stage, working alone is more effective than collaborating, although identifying and using a sounding board – ideally someone within your department who is familiar with your curriculum, cohort and vision – is invaluable. A trusted critical friend can bring their own perspective and a fresh pair of eyes, but it also works as a test of the overall coherence of your enquiry. Can you explain it to someone else succinctly and in a way that bears scrutiny? Use this critical friend frequently throughout; as well as improving your enquiry, it demonstrates trust in your colleagues and gives them a feeling of involvement in the project.

Assessing your enquiry

Deciding how to assess students' learning at the end of the enquiry is the last major hurdle that you will face, and ideally, this will be factored into the enquiry's initial construction. This need not be complicated: if the enquiry and its overarching question are good, simply asking students to answer that question is the purest test of learning and development that you can find. For our Year 9 enquiry, 'What does it mean to be British today?', our students are asked exactly that, and they frequently amaze us with the depth and range of their thinking and writing. If the enquiry is built around sources or material culture, then an assessment that challenges students to curate an exhibit on the topic, making selections and justifying those choices, is incredibly illuminating for how students have grasped the significance of these items and their connection to the story. Ultimately, whatever form the assessment takes, it should be as closely linked to the objective of the enquiry as possible.

You can find a case study on building a school visit around an enquiry from Jonathan Mountstevens on the online resource centre.

Summary

- Historical enquiries promote problem-solving and independent thinking and give students transferrable skills for life.

- Effective enquiry questions should focus on an aspect of disciplinary knowledge, be purposeful and relevant, allow for challenge and be interesting to students.

- A good historical enquiry will underpin an entire topic or unit.

- Enquiry questions give shape and coherence to the knowledge we teach.

- The enquiry question is a useful planning device, enabling teachers to research and then structure coherent sequences of lessons and build knowledge systematically.

- Students can be involved in writing enquiries.

- Avoid enquiries that strongly suggest a 'right' answer or that might encourage misconceptions.

- Revisit your enquiry question regularly – for example, once per lesson.

- You can create enquiries based around high-quality books.

- Enquiry questions can be used to provide a coherent structure and framework for trips.

PART 2

Delivering effective history lessons

5

Developing historical knowledge and skills

In this chapter, we look at how you can develop students' historical knowledge and their historical skills in the key areas of: causation, significance, evidence, interpretation, and change and continuity.

Knowledge

Knowledge is one of the biggest challenges that students face. They are constantly exposed to more of it each day, both in school and in their daily lives. Young people are learning facts from textbooks, but they are also learning knowledge from other people in conversation and experience, and they must endeavour to process and retain this knowledge. How can we make it stick?

'New' knowledge is often referred to as 'powerful knowledge' in academia. Powerful knowledge is knowledge that is different from our previous experiences (Young, 2013). It is the knowledge that can be combined with existing knowledge to help conversion to long-term memory. Converting working (or short-term) memory into long-term memory is a process that takes time and effort. Knowledge needs to be visited and revisited over time in order for it to be fully retained. The process of combining existing knowledge with new concepts in order to help new knowledge stick is outlined by Nuthall (2007).

In your classroom, this means choosing activities that integrate new knowledge with existing knowledge. This is more effective than simply learning lots of new knowledge because part of it is already familiar, and therefore the learning experience is less strenuous and more memorable for students.

There are a number of ways you can help students to integrate new and existing knowledge – for example, linking back to your enquiry question or 'big picture' regularly (see Chapter 10). Here are some other strategies you can try.

Identify existing knowledge

Before you can design activities to link new and existing knowledge, you need to know what students' existing knowledge is. All children come to school with existing knowledge of the world, even those on their first day in Reception. A teacher, therefore, must seek to identify this knowledge early on. A benefit of identifying existing student knowledge is that you can combat any myths or misinformation that a student might have learned. Common knowledge and popular culture can sometimes contradict historical fact, so a teacher must identify these misconceptions and correct them.

ADDRESSING MISCONCEPTIONS – WORLD WAR ONE AND TWO

A common example is that students often think that Hitler/the Nazis were to blame for World War One. When teaching the causes of World War One, a good activity is to begin with students writing down everything they think they know about it. It is common for students to mix information about World Wars One and Two, so this activity allows a teacher to address this. It can be a great learning moment when a student claims that Hitler started World War One. You can praise the student for giving this answer as it opens up conversation about why people often think this to be true. Discussion can then focus on the facts: how Hitler was a regular soldier in the German army, said to have little leadership ability; how the Nazi Party were created in 1920, after World War One; and how World War One was the summation of much more long-term tension, beyond the control of one mere person. Correcting prior knowledge can also help with knowledge retention, as students are then more likely to remember that the 'original' fact was wrong, and may even correct others in future.

Interleaving and cumulative assessments

Interleaving and cumulative assessments are methods of combining new and existing knowledge, and testing what the students have retained over time. The idea is to test existing knowledge alongside new knowledge, with questions from last lesson, last week, last month and (for exam classes) even from the previous year to see what students remember.

Knowledge retrieval tasks

Knowledge retention can become an issue as students approach their GCSE and A level exams, which place high emphasis on knowledge retrieval. This is commonly a struggle for many students, especially when retaining knowledge across a plethora of different subjects. Therefore, the ability of both teachers and students to practise knowledge retention and retrieval from an early stage is very important.

How can we address knowledge retrieval efficiently in lessons, given our restrictions on time? If all lesson time is spent on existing knowledge, little time will remain for learning new knowledge. Whilst new knowledge is often best learned by elaborating on existing knowledge, all of this is still rather time-consuming, and time is a luxury that teachers rarely have to spare.

One common strategy that can be effective is quick five- or ten-question fact tests, often at the beginning or end of lessons, to briefly identify what has been remembered and what has not. This low-stakes testing can help students and teachers alike to identify what knowledge has and has not been retained and can inform next steps for your lesson.

Alongside the traditional fact test, it can be beneficial to add another layer of knowledge retrieval, both as a stimulus to jog the memory and to ensure that students do not 'opt out' of fact retrieval due to lack of effort. An effective strategy is to include an image with accompanying questions, varying from 'What do you see in this photo?' through to questions about inference and reliability. By adding this, a teacher can give a range of challenge to students of varying abilities, and it limits students' opportunity to opt out of a task by claiming to have forgotten knowledge. Additionally, when selected carefully, the image and its questions may act as a prompt, helping a student who has genuinely forgotten knowledge to retrieve it more easily.

We discuss further knowledge retrieval ideas in Chapters 6 and 10.

Make it relatable

Knowledge is often easier to remember if it is relatable, as seen in the case study below.

TEACHING WORLD WAR TWO

Whilst teaching the events of World War Two, it is common to focus on the acts and experiences of the main countries involved, such as Britain, France, Germany and the USA. Whilst these key players were arguably most significant in shaping the course of events, other countries played significant roles too, but are often overlooked. Whilst teaching in a multicultural and multinational secondary school, I realised that many of the students would not be able to relate when teaching World War Two from a British point of view (as many schools and teachers commonly do). I decided to ask the students which countries they wanted to be included in a lesson I was planning about the key events of World War Two. I then found out about the roles of these countries, such as Guyana, Malta and the Philippines, before sharing it with the students. The students relished learning about 'their' countries and 'their' history, and it was a positive example to show myself as the teacher learning new information too. The knowledge was far more relatable for them, and their recall of it was excellent several lessons later. One parent, a few months later at parents evening, told me how their student came home and taught their family all about their country, and remembered the excitement with which they did this. This worked well because of the demographic in the classroom, which may not always be the case, but the point remains that knowledge is often easier to remember if it is relatable.

Note: this could have worked well as a research lesson, with students doing their own investigation into a country of their choice, but the school did not have adequate facilities for this, hence my doing it in this way instead.

Causation

People have always sought reasons for why things happen. We investigate people's motives and the explanations behind natural events to help us understand the event itself. Historians too seek to understand why stories play out the way they do, especially when even the smallest decisions can have big consequences. Carr cites causation as a key process for a historian (Carr, 2018).

At an early age, students can begin to learn the ideas of cause and consequence: there are reasons why things happen, and the things that happen have an impact. Later, they can learn that the consequences themselves can often become causes of the subsequent events, and so on. Initially, this creates a linear story of history, with one thing leading to another. As students mature in their studies of history, they will be able to see that often there are several factors at play that cause an event to happen, and a multitude of impacts that arise as a result. It is the job of the history teacher to help students understand how one action can lead to another.

Understanding the difference between long-term and short-term causes

A common issue when teaching causation is trying to help students understand the difference between long- and short-term causes. For many students, they think that the cause of an event is the thing that happened just before the event.

At its core, this is not incorrect, and at the beginning of a student's historical education, this is a good concept to learn. As students approach secondary school, it is important to move on from this, to understand that whilst the thing before the event (often referred to as the catalyst) is almost certainly an important cause, there may be other causes before it.

One of the difficulties in teaching this is that students often request a binary number or set period of time to allow them to quantify what is short-term and what is long-term. They might ask, 'Are the events in the weeks and months before a war short-term, and years before long-term?' This is a good question, as students are demonstrating they are trying to separate the two types of causes, but history is more nuanced. Historians do not really have a set 'number' that determines short- versus long-term, and it can vary by event, which makes it harder for younger students to manage.

When exploring causation, we look for factors that led to an event happening. By doing so, we can often see tensions building and actions getting more and more likely (especially in reference to human action). When the student knows about the resulting event, it can be tempting to create a scenario where the event was always going to happen. Students often then consider the event to be 'inevitable'. This is problematic, as no event is guaranteed to happen. Many events might have been very likely to happen, given the factors at play. However, to suggest that the events were guaranteed actually downplays the causes, as it suggests that the event would have happened anyway regardless of actions beforehand. Avoid use of the word 'inevitable'. Instead, try to quantify the likelihood of an event happening. This can be a very high-level thinking activity for students.

VISUALISING STEPS TO POWER

As part of a unit exploring Hitler's rise to power, I devised the activity in Figure 5.1 to help students understand how Hitler's power built over time. Aimed at Year 9, this symbolises a linear causation model; after creating this graph, we did discuss other influences on Hitler's power, to help students gain an awareness of other factors.

I taught students about each fact and then gave students the timeline of nine key events in Hitler's rise to power. I asked students to place each event on the graph, not only in chronological order, but also considering how much power Hitler gained at each point.

Pedagogically, this challenged students to give weight to the different causes, identifying which factors increased his power more than others. The graph then shows how Hitler's power increased over time. This task is an example of top-down teaching – by challenging all students to make decisions about the weight of importance of each cause, you challenge the highest-attaining students. Other students will be able to attempt this, and at the very least gain a sense of causation in terms of one event leading to another.

Hitler's steps to power

1. After World War One, Germany had many problems.
2. Hitler said he would create jobs and make Germany rich.
3. 1929, USA: Wall Street Crash.
4. Unemployment reached 6 million in Germany by 1932.
5. Hitler was a brilliant orator.
6. Many people voted for Hitler in the Reichstag (parliament) elections.
7. In January 1933, the old President Hindenburg made Hitler chancellor (prime minister).
8. February 1933: The Reichstag fire was blamed on the Communists.
9. Hitler bullied the Reichstag into passing the Enabling Act. This gave him power to do as he pleased.

FIGURE 5.1A: *Hitler's steps to power*

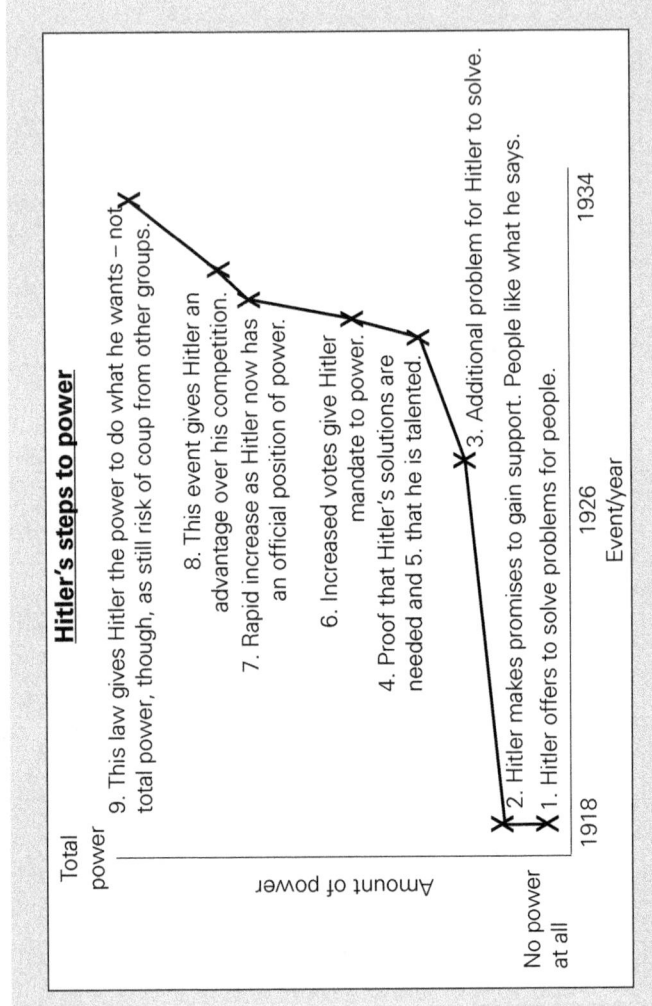

FIGURE 5.1B: *Hitler's steps to power*

Significance

In this section, we consider ways that you can develop your students' skills and understanding of significance.

Awareness of significance of topics

The significance of the history that we teach in the classroom is already implied – there is a reason why a particular topic has been selected for teaching; therefore it must be significant for some reason. Either it is featured on the National Curriculum, meaning the government considers it important, or the school history department has chosen it for their scheme of work. This selection process is extremely important, as discussed in Chapter 1.

The process of deciding what to include and what to omit is centred on significance, but students are generally left out of this decision-making, and so are unaware of why they are studying certain topics. Students should have an awareness of why they are studying something, beyond the surface 'because my teacher said so' response.

The problem is that evaluating the significance of something requires an awful lot of historical knowledge, not just about that event or person, but about others too. This allows the historian to compare the relative short- and long-term significance of the topic. Many students simply do not yet have enough knowledge to be able to make such decisions, especially younger students. However, this does not mean they cannot be part of conversations about why certain topics are chosen. Indeed, giving students the National Curriculum after having studied some topics and asking them to consider why the government chose them can be quite a powerful reflection task.

Significance of people

Students can begin to learn to evaluate significance on a smaller scale at the end of a scheme of work. Determining the significance of a particular person is often easiest. You can have conversations with students about what that person did or did not do, and what was notable.

Using the word 'significant'

Using the word 'significant' is imperative. Often, students need you to translate the word to 'important' at first, but using the original language is best after this, both for exams that discuss significance and for future studies of history.

The five Rs

Several frameworks exist for teachers to help them guide students in their studies of significance. The most notable framework is Christine Counsell's 'five Rs'. Using these criteria allows students to question whether an event or person was 'Remarkable, Remembered, Resulted in change, Resonant or Revealing' (Counsell, 2004), before coming to an overall conclusion on its significance. This can also help determine what is *not* significant. With younger students, teachers might use one or two of the criteria, but as students develop in their skills, they can not only use all five, but also compare them to create a complex understanding of significance.

Evidence

Evidence is one of the most crucial features in the study of the past. Frequently, when recounting stories of events and people to students, teachers are asked how they *know* that this is what happened. What proof is there that this happened? This tends to lead to excellent conversations about different types of evidence that historians use to support their hypotheses, and how reliable or useful each piece of evidence is to a historian.

Grouping evidence

Some students consider evidence individually, rather than combining evidence as part of an enquiry. Try to help students see that historians use various pieces of evidence as a group in order to prove a theory.

Reliability of evidence

One question that students must learn to ask of a piece of evidence is how reliable it is. Can a historian trust the evidence to be accurate? Initially, some students struggle with this, as they consider evidence to be full of facts that *must* be true, especially if it is something that has come from an authoritative person (e.g. evidence from a prime minister).

It is the teacher's job to encourage students to question content, and not to believe that everything they see or read is completely true. Unfortunately, whilst encouraging students to question the reliability of the content of sources, sometimes students can then do the opposite, disregarding any information in a source as made up by the person who wrote it. Striking the balance between these two viewpoints, and being able to understand how much to trust a source, is what the teacher is aiming for.

From experience, giving students examples can often help. For example, if you read a source that said what an amazing leader Hitler was, but it was written by a leading Nazi, it would be considered less reliable, as the Nazi would have a reason for wanting Hitler to seem amazing. Similarly, if you were using some evidence about an event from someone who was not involved but was an eyewitness, you would consider this to be quite reliable, as the person was there at the time but may not have reason to lie or exaggerate.

Understanding how reliable evidence is to a historian is also a useful life skill, helping students to question what they see or hear in the news or social media.

Usefulness of evidence

Linked to this is the concept of usefulness. Many GCSE papers ask history students to evaluate the usefulness of a source of information. Students are required to be able to consider various aspects of the evidence, such as who wrote it, when they wrote it and why they wrote it, to be able to determine whether it is useful to a historian. Many students begin with a rather binary approach to this, judging sources to be either completely amazing or completely useless. In reality, neither is true: very few sources of information are completely useless or so useful that they are not flawed. Rather, usefulness should be considered as a spectrum, with the determining factor being the enquiry of the historian.

Again, examples are helpful here, particularly silly ones. For example, a historian studying the War of the Roses would find evidence about Henry VII to be *quite* useful, but evidence about Queen Elizabeth II would be far *less* useful. Alternatively, a piece of evidence about whiteboard markers would not be useful if studying World War Two, but could be *slightly* useful for a historian studying the history of stationery. This helps students to see that all evidence can be useful, dependent on the enquiry of the historian. Teachers should note the use of quantitative words such as 'slightly' and 'quite', which indicate a student's ability to evaluate the usefulness of evidence.

CRUSADES EVIDENCE WORKSHEET

Using a quote from a speech, the worksheet in Figure 5.2 helps students to analyse evidence in a step-by-step manner.

The source is placed in the middle of the worksheet. There are various questions with answer boxes, each designed to help students understand the piece of evidence and encourage them to challenge it. The worksheet allows students of varying abilities to access the evidence, ranging from key words to support students who might find the language in the evidence difficult, to an extension question (which would require the use of some prior knowledge too). Printed on a single page, this task differentiates by outcomes, but allows all learners to develop the skill of analysing evidence.

Why did people go on Crusade?

Year 7: Source analysis Why did people go on Crusades?	What is the source about? (What is the source trying to say?)	
Who said this? Why is this person important? Why would it be different if a peasant said these words?	[source]	**Key words:** Crusade: a war for the Holy Land between Muslims and Christians during the medieval period Saracens: a medieval word for Muslims Foul: disgusting, horrible Infidel: people who do not believe in Christianity Bandits: people who rob or steal Pope: a person who is the leader of the Catholic Church
	Speech by Pope Urban II, 1095	
What reasons does the source give for going on a Crusade?	**Extension: Why is it important that the source was written in 1095?**	

FIGURE 5.2: *Crusades evidence worksheet*

Interpretation

Skills around evidence are closely linked to skills centred around interpretation. A historical interpretation can be described as an account that someone has created of the past, based on the evidence that they have found. To students, this can often be seen as synonymous with evidence, as they often view what historians think as factual and true. Students often see historians' accounts as evidence of what happened, and do not feel they can agree or disagree with what a historian has said.

Whilst it is good that students respect the work of historians, it is not ideal that students do not feel they can challenge them. Indeed, if all historians accepted the work of those before them to be 100 per cent accurate and true, there would be many misconceptions in history. The work of a historian is to check that the stories that we have of the past are indeed accurate and true, and to do so they must challenge what we already know; teachers must therefore encourage students to do the same.

It can be useful to think of interpretations as a *judgement* of the past – a constructed narrative that has taken into account various pieces of evidence and is as accurate as is possible at the time of writing. The use of the word 'opinion' is best avoided, as it does not emphasise that their judgement is based on historical evidence. Highlight the idea that it is as accurate as possible; after publication, more evidence might come to light that the historian did not have access to, which might change the accuracy of their interpretation. It is crucial to encourage students to understand the changing nature of interpretations and their relationship with historical evidence.

Historiographical interpretations

You can find many interpretations in historians' academic writing. Reading books by historians is beneficial to students for many reasons: it encourages reading (which is often a priority for schools), develops an understanding of the role of a historian and outlines the interpretation in the historian's own words. You can select a contrasting viewpoint from another academic source and then ask students to compare the two views. Or you can ask students to complete a book report or an extract analysis. There are more suggestions on ways to use academic writing in Chapter 6.

Change and continuity

When students consider change and continuity, they need to organise the knowledge they have learned. Comparing contrasting themes helps students to see what has stayed the same over a period of time and what has changed. This can be helpful for students to identify periods of calm and peace, as well as when turbulent events may be building.

At a more complex level, students might be asked to consider the pace of change, extent of change or type of change. Many GCSE specifications have an entire unit focused around these aspects.

Crafting enquiry questions carefully

Consider the enquiry question carefully when exploring change and continuity. Questions that begin simply with 'Why…?' may actually generate an answer that is more closely related to causation rather than change (though the two are often interlinked). Instead, try questions that ask 'How far...?' or 'To what extent...?', which inherently lead to a more nuanced answer. Questions that include a time period are also good, as change and continuity within that period can be discussed. Enquiry questions are discussed in more detail in Chapter 4.

Visualising change and continuity

Visualising change and continuity is very helpful for many students. Graphs are particularly good for this. Visual representations can benefit many learners, as they offer an accessible way into the concept. However, they are also great for adding challenge for students, e.g. to identify turning points and key moments within history, where things change rapidly or significantly.

Summary

- Knowledge is one of the biggest challenges that students face.

- New knowledge should be combined with existing knowledge so that it can be retained in students' long-term memories.

- It is important to identify existing knowledge and address misconceptions.

- New and existing knowledge can be combined by referring to enquiry questions, using interleaving, cumulative assessments, knowledge retrieval tasks and making the knowledge relatable.

- When teaching causation, help students to understand the difference between long-term and short-term causes.

- When teaching significance, make sure to use the word 'significant', consider using frameworks like the five Rs, begin by looking at the significance of a person and perhaps ask students to consider the significance of topics on the curriculum.

- When teaching evidence skills, ensure that students do not just consider pieces of evidence individually. Give students examples of reliable and unreliable evidence, as well as useful and less useful evidence.

- You can teach students to analyse evidence by giving them step-by-step support.

- When teaching interpretations, it can be helpful to explain that interpretations are judgements of the past.

- You can use historians' academic writing to teach interpretations.

- When teaching change and continuity, craft your enquiry questions carefully and consider representing change and continuity visually to help your students.

6

Key strategies for the history classroom

In this chapter, we are going to look at the following history teaching strategies that underpin other chapters in this book:

- retrieval practice
- modelling and metacognition
- reading and comprehension development
- extended writing skills training.

Retrieval practice

The benefits of retrieval practice have been studied for many years. Here are some suggestions for effective implementation of retrieval practice in your teaching of history. I also discuss retrieval starters in Chapter 10.

Establish what you want students to remember

What I often do is work backwards by analysing exam questions and creating various possible future exam questions. I use these questions to establish the core knowledge students need to know to be able to answer exam questions and access new knowledge throughout the course. I can then use this information to plan retrieval practice.

Quizzes

Create quizzes that enable students to develop their disciplinary thinking as well as specific knowledge like dates and statistics. Questions such as 'Which of these statements help explain the impact of migrants in the industrial period?' allow students to recall and draw upon a wide range of knowledge, as well as give them the opportunity to practise the discipline of causation. In this way, we can use retrieval practice as an active process of making meaning.

Source work

Source work is a form of retrieval practice, because students need knowledge to contextualise the sources they are seeing. I frame this as: 'Which source would you use for an enquiry into X and why?' It is important that we expose our students to as many sources as possible, even for topics where sources are not on the paper, to ensure that practice is regular and confidence grows. Source work is the foundation of the discipline of history; therefore, it is important that students practise this skill.

Timeline tests

This activity encourages students to engage in chronological thinking, as they have to recall and place events in the correct order. This is an effective activity as it mirrors the retrieval processes that students need in an exam. Therefore, I commonly use this activity before the class plans a narrative question. As a challenge task, I ask students to explain the links between the events or explain how one event contributes to or leads to another. This helps students to see the relationship between different parts of their knowledge on a topic, rather than seeing them as isolated parts.

Support the point

Point to an exam question on the board and invite students to contribute two or three pieces of evidence or knowledge to support their answer. This helps students to recall relevant knowledge.

Match the interpretation with own knowledge

Note a specific historian's viewpoint about a certain topic or event on the board using a quote. Ask students to support that quote with two or three pieces of knowledge. This again mirrors the thinking skills and processes students will need for their exam, especially exam questions where students are asked how far they agree with an interpretation.

Graphic retrieval tasks

Display an exam question on the board and ask students to answer it by creating a graphic representation, using arrows to show links and relationships between events. This is a quicker way of assessing their retrieval than a long essay.

What connects these factors?

Place various categories of factors or events on the board and ask students to connect similar factors or events together and then explain why they have connected them. This activity supports retrieval practice, provides insight into how students make meaning of knowledge, and reveals connections between knowledge.

Modelling and metacognition

If you want to teach someone how to make spaghetti Bolognese well, you do not present them with the finished dish without letting them see how you prepared it. You would instead guide them through the process, explaining at various points and then demonstrating. The history essay is our spaghetti Bolognese: historical writing is a form of disciplinary knowledge that we must teach our students. As practitioners, we should use modelling and metacognition to make the process of excellence explicit to students so that they can replicate the same pattern and thinking. Modelling should aid our explanations. We need to recognise the particularities of historical writing and show our students how to replicate them.

Modelling should be inherent in everything we do. For example, I use modelling to set up tasks: as a class, we complete the first part of a table together; this gives students a demonstrated example through my verbal explanations, which increases their confidence to be able to do the task independently, which in turn improves behaviour as well as clarity on how their work should be presented.

Nevertheless, this section will focus on modelling to improve historical writing.

There are a number of different question styles for our history students to cope with at KS4 and KS5; it can become overwhelming for them. Therefore, we need to help build their confidence to tackle these. Modelling and metacognition can be our best friend here. Breaking components of answers into manageable chunks and then demonstrating to students how to put those chunks together is an effective strategy to help improve outcomes and achieve mastery.

Source skills

When writing about sources, students can find it difficult to analyse the utility and reliability of sources, and to make inferences from them. This is because there are several thinking components at play:

- understanding the sources
- understanding their context
- placing the sources into contextual knowledge of the time period
- understanding the specific focus of the question
- writing in a coherent and logical manner that communicates these various understandings.

We need to support students in how best to tackle historical writing in its different forms and weave various elements of thinking together into a coherent, well-structured manner.

Thinking strategies

Before modelling how to write, we should first model how to think about writing. Here we return to the principle of metacognition. We should strive to develop our students' ability to think about the discipline of history in the way that we do as the experts. We must explicitly teach our thinking strategies if we want our students to employ them.

For students to develop their metacognitive abilities and to effectively plan, monitor and evaluate their learning, they need to possess three types of content knowledge:

- declarative knowledge – facts you can say or declare are true

- procedural knowledge – how to perform the process step by step

- conditional knowledge – knowing when to use a procedure, skill or strategy, and when not to use it.

When approaching an exam question, as experts it is important to share our thinking with students, so that they can employ the relevant thinking strategies.

Pre-planned answer

To be able to support our students to write the best responses, we ourselves need to know how to get from start to finish and be prepared to model each section first and then complete the answer. Therefore, I typically write out an A* or Grade 9 response for myself, then annotate my thinking. This helps me to live model my thinking process to students and show how I got to the product.

I typically keep my pre-planned answer with annotations beside my visualiser for reference, to aid my explanations in class during my live demonstration. My pre-planned answer acts as a script and provides a sense of security for me. I keep these pre-planned answers or modelling scripts within my 'modelling book', which I keep for the following years, to aid with the teaching of the next cohort.

Live annotation under a visualiser

You can annotate a source under a visualiser or on your whiteboard with all the thoughts you have whilst trying to understand its relevance and meaning. This enables students to see the process of breaking down the thinking and procedural elements:

- What do you see? What does it say?

- What does that suggest?

- What do you know that supports that?

- What is helpful or unhelpful about the nature of the source?

- Who produced the source? Why might that be a helpful or unhelpful thing?

- When was the source produced? Why might that be a helpful or unhelpful thing?

- Where was the source produced? Why might that be a helpful or unhelpful thing?

- Why do you think the source might have been produced? Why might that be a helpful or unhelpful thing?

By consistently asking the above sort of question when evaluating sources, we provide a scaffold for students to be able to evaluate sources independently.

Tracing paper annotation

Give your students tracing paper to cover a past paper. Ask them to annotate on the tracing paper with their thinking. Then ask them to remove the tracing paper and complete the answers. You can also use 'spaced practice' and leave a few days between students exploring the questions and answering them.

Live modelling

When live modelling, I sometimes get students to copy down what I am writing. However, this can mean that they are only engaging passively. Therefore, sometimes I ask them to watch the live construction, as this can help them cognitively engage with the process. I might say something like: 'Pens down, full attention on what we are doing together.' Remember there is power in the thinking, not just the doing. Emphasise to students that it is important to understand the process and ask them to contribute or challenge. This can make for pivotal moments in the classroom.

Dual coding and modelling

The theory of dual coding suggests that cognition is divided into two processing systems: visual and verbal. In practice, this means explaining using both words and images. When it comes to explaining to students the causes and consequences of historical events or developing their analysis of the types and pace of change, dual coding can be a good strategy to use. This can include using a visualiser to draw a concept whilst you explain it or showing a diagram and talking through it. Caviglioli and Goodwin's book *Organise Ideas: Thinking* by Hand, *Extending the Mind* (2021) provides useful ideas for these sorts of strategies. If you would like to see dual coding and modelling in action within a history classroom, Ben Newmark's YouTube videos are an excellent example of marrying up dual coding with concise explanations and storytelling.

Silent modelling

Sometimes a teacher talking during a demonstration can distract students from learning from the process. Silent modelling allows for thoughtful engagement without the cognitive overload of teacher talk. As a result, students' focus can be much more intense.

Modelling historical writing at KS5

Teaching KS5 history students to write academically can be hard, due to the leap they have to make from KS4 to KS5. They also have to apply subject knowledge and disciplinary skills and express these in written form. At KS5, unlike other key stages, the challenge is to create independent learners ready for university, whilst still providing adequate support and without 'spoon-feeding'.

I became an examiner in 2018, after the launch of the new A level. This became an invaluable experience for me, particularly in terms of deeply understanding the exam board expectations. Not only did this increase my understanding of how students should apply their knowledge, but it also built my confidence in teaching the new A level, and in particular live modelling, because I thoroughly understood what the exam board was looking for.

The fear with live modelling at KS5 is that students may become dependent on me, the expert. Research shows that the use of modelling should move from guided practice to independent practice (see, for example, Rosenshine, 2012). As a result, every Friday, students would have a live modelling seminar. Each seminar focused on a particular skill, e.g.:

- week 1: structure
- week 2: writing an A* introduction
- week 3: selecting accurate, relevant and precise evidence
- week 4: developing explanations, analysis and evaluation
- week 5: sustaining judgements after acknowledging an opposing argument to their judgement
- week 6: writing an A* conclusion
- week 7: merging the skills together.

Each seminar encompassed:

- a knowledge quiz
- live modelling a paragraph from the expert, whereby I made the implicit explicit
- joint construction of a paragraph from the students and expert
- independent practice with the exact same question
- independent practice with a similar question but different wording.

As students became experts in term 2, I started introducing them to academic literature, in order for the students to learn from historians' styles, constructions and language. We studied vast amounts of historian construction through an activity called 'zoning' (breaking down their construction using a visualiser). Some students said that this helped to bridge the gap between A level and university.

Reading and comprehension development

Studying history involves a lot of reading. This can be reading from textbooks, historical scholarship, sources and information sheets that teachers produce. Reading and comprehension development is therefore important. Developing this skill can involve teaching a range of techniques, including:

- inferring meaning from context
- summarising or identifying key points
- using graphic or semantic organisers
- developing questioning strategies
- monitoring their own comprehension, then identifying and resolving difficulties for themselves.

In successful reading comprehension approaches, teachers carefully tailor activities to students' reading capabilities, and involve activities and texts that provide an effective, but not overwhelming, challenge. Some students with learning differences may struggle with this aspect in particular, and may need additional intervention strategies (see Chapter 9).

Pre-teach vocabulary

Identify words your students are unlikely to know and systematically 'pre-teach' them. Tom Hopkins-Burke provides a great case study in Chapter 10 with ideas on how to do this. You can also try using repetition with the class or brief quizzes using the words in different contexts.

Read aloud yourself

You can read from a textbook, a children's history book, children's historical fiction or maybe even a short section of academic writing. Make sure the passage is well-written. You and your students will be able to enjoy it as well as learn from it.

Find cliffhangers

Try reading aloud and then stopping at a cliffhanger to create a desire to read independently.

Write your own stories

You might not always be able to find the story you need for your particular lesson. One solution might be to write your own. See Chapter 8 for more ideas on using stories.

Tell the story first in a more accessible way

This idea is the opposite of the idea above about cliffhangers. Sometimes, it is best if students know the story, direction or interesting features first, so that they can move into grasping where it is all going and why. This is often the case with otherwise complex primary sources.

Extended writing skills training

Writing is fundamental to the study of history. In fact, it is the main way in which we assess students' understanding of the past. Therefore, developing our student's writing is central to history teaching.

For many of our students, extended writing is difficult. It is a challenge to recall knowledge, select the knowledge that is relevant to the question, organise the knowledge and then write. In the exam, they have to do all this in timed conditions.

Here are some suggestions for ways to develop your students' extended writing skills.

Find and fix

Give students a paragraph to correct (a 'find and fix paragraph'). This allows for targeted essay practice: spot the mistake in the structure, improve the analysis, check whether the right facts been selected, etc. The sample answers in examiner reports are useful for this because there are plenty of pre-written paragraphs to choose from, usually of varying quality, and you can add a few mistakes as you type them.

Spider diagrams

Start planning essays as a whole-class activity using spider diagrams. Give students a blank sheet of paper (replicating the GCSE exam conditions). Ask students to write the question in the centre of the page. Then ask them to identify the four big points they are going to make to answer the question and put these around the question as 'legs'. They can then add the detailed knowledge that they are going to use to back up their point around each 'leg'. Finally, they can add one last leg to the spider with their conclusion.

Once we have done a couple of these as a class, students have a go at a different essay question on their own. I collect in the plans before they write so that I can check them and see whether they have selected relevant points and evidence. Once I have given feedback on this stage, students are able to have a go at writing the essay themselves. By marking the plan before they write, I am able to give support and guidance to students who are missing the point of the question. The first essay they write can then be focused and clear.

Dialogue before writing – oracy

Giving students the opportunity to discuss, explain and develop their ideas orally before committing pen to paper can be a huge confidence boost and helps them to clarify their thinking before they start to write. Oral discussion sometimes helps students see the point of writing; it can even make them hungry to write.

Debates are also a useful activity to help students see the importance of using precise examples to back up their points, as well as realising the importance of coming back to the question once you have made your point so that you can explain just how central or otherwise the argument is to the question. Encourage students to prepare for a debate on a particular topic. This can act as an 'oral rehearsal', where ideas about selection, organisation or wording are tried out and honed in a low-stakes way before a higher-stakes essay.

Historian extracts

Students should be hearing or reading rich, inspiring academic prose by the master-craftspeople themselves, historians. This in turn exposes students to articulating an argument.

Many teachers have used scholarship explicitly to teach writing. Look for stylistic features of a particular historian and then read aloud from that historian (slowly and dramatically). Ask students to listen out or look out for the features you have highlighted.

Good topic knowledge

Regular retrieval practice will allow students to develop fluent recall of essential information. Checking for knowledge and understanding before students independently write can reduce the amount of time students use to remember whilst trying to maintain their line of reasoning. For our KS3 assessments, we typically have two parts: Part 1 is a quiz; Part 2 is the extended writing (see Chapter 2 for further details on this).

Make it visual

Encourage students to create cards or digital cards out of different parts of an essay so that they can then play around with them, select the appropriate information and organise it to create a sensible order that works for a particular task or question.

Allow free-flowing writing

Allow your students to put their claims, arguments and thoughts into words, writing their ideas freely, perhaps just with an initial sentence to work with. Use this initial outpouring of ideas as a rough draft and then teach students to edit their work.

Summary

- Four key strategies that will underpin much of your history teaching are retrieval practice, modelling and metacognition, reading and comprehension development, and extended writing skills training.

- Implementing these strategies regularly in your teaching will equip your students with the skills needed to analyse materials, develop understanding and write clearly.

7

Feedback

Marking is *not* always feedback. In many schools, the terms 'feedback' and 'marking' have been used interchangeably. Marking is often part of a high-stakes accountability process to show pupil progress. Meeting the requirements of a marking policy does not necessarily equate to influencing student learning, yet it does increase workload. We must adopt approaches to feedback that have a low impact on teacher workload but a high impact on student learning, development and improvement.

Effective feedback can contribute to the development of historical thinking skills, critical analysis and a deeper understanding of complex historical concepts and events. Feedback that guides students in evaluating sources, constructing interpretations and engaging with evidence can enhance their overall learning experience in history education.

Approaches to effective feedback

The Education Endowment Foundation published key guidance on effective feedback: 'Teacher feedback to improve pupil learning.' In their report, they identify three fundamental principles for teachers to follow:

1. 'Lay the foundations for effective feedback, with high-quality initial teaching that includes careful formative assessment;

2. deliver appropriately-timed feedback, that focuses on moving learning forward; and, crucially,

3. plan for how pupils will receive and use feedback using strategies to ensure that pupils will act on the feedback offered.' (Collin and Quigley, 2021, p. 4)

Live feedback

Live feedback allows us to give students guidance in the moment, to help them towards success. It can reveal any underlying misconceptions and reduce the potential to have to pick up these points after the work has been completed.

You can provide live feedback by circulating the room and checking students' work. Whilst circulating, you can jot down in your notebook any common misconceptions and then pause the independent activity to offer the whole class verbal feedback before they continue. Alternatively, you can offer feedback by writing questions or sentence starters in the margin of students' work whilst they are completing a task or extended writing. Common phrases or questions that I write as part of live feedback for extended writing are:

- Why?
- This is because…
- Add quote.
- Impact?
- An additional piece of evidence is…

- A dissenting view might point to…

- On balance, however…

- Link back to the question.

- Thus, we must assert…

- Why did you select this quote/evidence to support your claim/point?

This allows us to steer students back on track to reduce any potential procedural errors. After offering live feedback, whether that is verbal or written, we must return to circulating or to the particular student after a few minutes to check that they have acted on the feedback. Returning also shows students that you are committed to the feedback process.

Whole-class feedback

Whole-class feedback involves providing feedback on a piece of work to the whole class at the same time. I typically use it for summative assessment or mock exams. One of the problems I found when I initially used whole-class feedback was that students struggled to see what statements within the crib sheet applied to them. I therefore adopted Andy Atherton's (@_codexterous) approach to whole-class feedback. His approach is the following:

- Highlight what you like – as you read student work, use a highlighter to highlight examples of good work. This helps to show students that you have read and paid attention to their work, as well as playing an important metacognitive role later in the feedback process.

- Find common misconceptions – whilst reading students' work, consider patterns of misconceptions across the class that you can reteach. This itself is a highly valuable use of a feedback lesson.

- Find examples of excellence – pinpoint several examples of excellence so that you can find and then share and live model the procedure of how to get there.

- Create a shareable template – collate and print a student-friendly version of your feedback. This could include a numbered list of next steps or targets, based on the common misconceptions you identified whilst reading students' work. Ensure your template has a space for a 'together task', e.g. a class construction of a better answer or paragraph, for all to complete in the feedback lesson.

Then, during the feedback session:

- Ask students what they did well – ask students to reread their work and pay attention to what you have highlighted. Ask students to consider why they think it is highlighted and what it is they are doing well (metacognition).

- Share excellent examples – live model and celebrate the examples of excellence you have identified (see modelling ideas in Chapter 6). The idea is to show what meeting the targets look like in action.

- Complete the together task – ask all students to complete the class 'together task' (see above) that will move everyone forward. (Adapted from Atherton, 2021)

PUTTING WHOLE-CLASS FEEDBACK INTO PRACTICE

Hannah McInroy-Betts, Head of Humanities

Our faculty has often grappled with how to get students to respond to feedback in a meaningful way. Our students tend to see a marked piece of work as complete. They see it as the end of the process and expect to move on. Yet, for the most part, the feedback that teachers give is formative and we want students to engage with it to make progress. In addition to this, the 'age-old' problem of finding the time to mark multiple pieces of written work in detail is compounded if all the students do is give the painstakingly written – and usually repetitive – comments a cursory glance. Therefore, our faculty has been experimenting with ways of delivering whole-class feedback that allow teachers to monitor student participation more easily and give little opportunity for students to opt out of a task, alongside improving the efficiency of marking.

To carry out a targeted whole-class feedback task, I read the student responses to a question and pick out the common strengths and development points. I put these into presentation slides and emphasise the strengths that most students have first, sometimes picking out examples of individuals who have done well. I publicly praise these students – if I know they will respond well to this – and choose sections of their answer to display. This can be a photograph if you want to make the process quicker or you can type out quotes if you want to anonymise it. I find that students respond well to the recognition of their hard work, and this personalises the process in the way that individual written comments usually would.

Secondly, I explain the common development points of the piece of work. Usually these are similar across a year group, especially in the early stages of student independent practice, so can be used both by other teachers in the faculty and in future years. To demonstrate what an exemplar answer would look like, I occasionally show a worked example, although I have found it increasingly effective to use live modelling, which allows the students to hear my thought process and gives them the opportunity to contribute to the exemplar if I pose a question to the class.

Structure strips can provide a scaffold – which will eventually be removed – that make it clear to students what needs to go in a paragraph or answer. In the AQA GCSE history exams, there are multiple question types that students need to master, each with quite a specific set of criteria. We found that students struggled to remember what to do in each question, so created a range of structure strips to help them in the more difficult questions.

For the first paragraph, I walk students through each step, verbalising aloud the thought process behind each part. I model what I would put, ask students what they would change or add, and students write their own version of the same point. I supplement this with a 'menu' of facts that they could select from to substantiate their point. Most students end up with a similar first paragraph. In the second paragraph, however, students tend to be more independent, using the model and the structure strips to guide them. The result in our class was that all students met the criteria in their second attempt and felt more confident when tackling a similar question in the future.

This is a feedback routine that we use consistently with our students in the faculty, and it has led to more time-efficient marking, more valuable student responses to feedback and an increase in student confidence when tackling a piece of writing. The routine is particularly effective when giving feedback after a mock, where it would be impossible to write comments on each question. At times, this approach does need to be modified slightly, particularly as some students become more familiar with the question stems or if you have a student who is particularly able. In this instance, I give the student more personalised feedback to ensure that they are challenged and I will spend some time with them in the lesson to explain what I mean. Overall, however, I am a strong advocate for whole-class feedback and the benefits it brings to both teachers and students.

Feedback grids

One year, my target as head of department (HOD) was to ensure that my department was consistently doing feedback lessons after a summative assessment, especially at KS3. One of the ways I ensured we did this was by creating and asking staff to create feedback grids for each assessment in KS3.

The feedback grid might look something like Figure 7.1. We present a model paragraph answer alongside the feedback grid in order to show students what their targets look like in action. During the feedback lesson, the teacher can annotate the model paragraph under the visualiser to show how it is

WWW (what went well)	EBI (even better if)
Your answer is well structured.	Ensure your essay is organised.
You have selected accurate, precise and relevant knowledge to use in each paragraph.	Select accurate and relevant own knowledge/detail to support your points in your paragraph.
You have used lots of specific own knowledge to support your points (Statistics, People, Events, Dates, Acts).	Try to use at least two or three pieces of specific knowledge (SPEDA) as evidence to support your points.
You have explained both the positive and negative impacts of colonialism consistently for each country.	Develop explanation of the impact of colonialism. Ensure that you explain both the positives and negatives.
You have explained how one experience is similar or different to another.	Ensure you consistently explain how one experience is similar or different to another.
You have a well-developed conclusion.	Develop your conclusion and explanations of comparisons by adding knowledge examples.

FIGURE 7.1: *Example feedback grid*

an example of excellence. We sometimes also give students a copy of the feedback grid and the model paragraph, with space underneath for them to rewrite their own paragraph. For KS3 students, I guide them to the paragraph(s) that they need to rewrite by placing an asterisk next to their weakest paragraph(s). This creates a standard and expectation of improvement. Students are unlikely to benefit from feedback unless time is set aside for them to reflect and act upon it. The grid provides a uniform and consistent approach within our department.

Elements to include in feedback

Feedback focuses on providing information on current performance based on how well the person has met the intentions of the task set. However, for improvement, we need to know how to engage with the feedback provided. Modelling and explicit instruction can enable students to act on feedback.

Helpful elements to include in feedback lessons might include:

- Asking students to complete a self-reflection sheet.

- Going through the questions that had the weakest answers.

- Live modelling under a visualiser or on a word-processed document to show how to reach a target. For example, instead of writing 'develop your explanations', I would annotate a piece of evidence that they used and pose one of the following questions: 'What is the impact of this?' or 'What is the impact of this in relation to your point?' Written questions enable students to engage easily with the feedback, rather than posing a statement.

- Using lots of the 'I do, we do, you do' approach (see Chapter 9) in order for students to explicitly see what their feedback looks like in action.

You can see examples of feedback lessons I delivered after Year 11 mocks on the online resource centre.

FURTHER READING

Here are some studies and insights on the subject of feedback in history teaching for further reading.

- The Historical Association website onebighistory department.com is an excellent source of information. See Martin Bajkowski's blog on the return to formal assessment at KS3 in history, 'Assessment at KS3 in history' (2023).

- 'Peering at history through different lenses: the role of disciplinary perspectives in teaching history' by Wineburg and Wilson (1988). Wineburg and Wilson's study highlights that explicit instruction and feedback on source evaluation significantly improves students' ability to evaluate sources.

- 'Confronting history's interpretive paradox while teaching fifth graders to investigate the past' by VanSledright (2002). VanSledright's research demonstrates that structured feedback that guides students' historical inquiry and interpretation can enhance their understanding of historical concepts and events.

- 'A scaffold, not a cage: progression and progression models in history' by Lee and Shemilt (2003). Lee and Shemilt highlight that formative assessment practices, including timely feedback, can improve students' historical understanding and their ability to analyse evidence.

- *Teaching WalkThrus* by Sherrington and Caviglioli (2020). This book provides a detailed explanation of how to live model effectively.

- 'To make sure your students are ready to practise, use mini-whiteboards' is a helpful a podcast by Adam Boxer (2022).

Summary

- Marking is not always feedback.

- We want to aim for feedback that has a high impact on student learning and a low impact on our workload.

- Effective feedback can contribute to the development of important historical skills.

- Careful formative assessment helps to lay the right foundations for effective feedback.

- Feedback needs to be appropriately timed and move learning forward.

- We need to plan for how pupils will act on feedback.

- Live feedback involves giving students guidance in the moment, during a lesson.

- Whole-class feedback can be particularly useful when looking at summative assessments.

- Feedback grids can offer consistency and accountability in providing feedback and ensuring students engage with it.

- Feedback lessons might include using self-reflection sheets, going through weakest answers, live modelling or the 'I do, we do, you do' approach.

8

Storytelling

Storytelling is a key tool for cultivating understanding in any lesson, be it KS3, KS4 or KS5. The lesson itself can be an 'unfolding story'. I fell in love with history due to the stories and cliffhangers but storytelling seems to have become a dying art.

Stories make knowledge memorable, exciting and nourishing and our subject lends itself well to stories. When we use stories, we work with the way the brain most likes to organise information and create networks of connected ideas. Storytelling helps to humanise the past. Unlike involved explanations or detailed arguments, everyone can relate to stories. Stories allow human minds to explore vast social networks and to build imagined communities far beyond the borders of their local social group. Stories provide opportunity for humour, fascination and curiosity. They highlight perennial qualities of human nature.

Despite their common derivation, the words 'history' and 'story' can suggest very different kinds of knowledge. 'History' can suggest a detached understanding of the past, whereas 'story' suggests thinking about individuals and their personal journeys. Whilst these differences can sometimes make the relationship between story and history uncomfortable, story remains fundamental to the way that we understand the world in which we live, and in this chapter, we will explore how we can use storytelling to teach history.

Why storytelling?

Jonathan Grande blogs about not solely relying on retrieval practice as an isolated teaching activity to make content memorable. He says: 'Reliance on retrieval practice can, I think, blind us. Blind us to the missed opportunities to make the content more memorable from its *very first teaching*.' (Grande, 2023) He goes on to write that telling 'great stories that run over a sequence of lessons' helps to make learning more memorable.

Students do not learn isolated pieces of knowledge; they learn by assimilating their new knowledge into their existing knowledge (see the concept of 'powerful knowledge' discussed in Chapter 5). Stories help to prevent information being imparted as atomised facts. Schank and Abelson (1995) present an overview of knowledge and memory in their research, emphasising the role of stories in structuring information, creating connections and facilitating better retention and recall.

Overall, psychological research consistently shows that storytelling plays a crucial role in memory and retention processes. It enhances engagement, directs attention, facilitates comprehension and inference-making, and aids in the construction of coherent mental representations, all of which contribute to better memory encoding and retention of information.

In essence, stories have both curricular and pedagogical power, as Ofsted recognised in its research review: 'Stories provide an organising framework for knowledge… In stories, the connections between parts, and between parts and the whole, are often clear – this connects potentially disparate or abstract ideas into a coherent whole. Stories exemplify complex and abstract ideas in meaningful, human-scale ways.' (Ofsted, 2021)

How to create a story

Creating historical stories involves a combination of research, imagination and attention to detail. Creating a historical narrative is not like creating an information sheet of facts. The narrative should have vivid descriptions of flavour, colour, smell, emotions, etc. Here are some steps to guide you in creating compelling historical stories.

1. **Choose your time period and setting:** Decide on the historical era you want to explore and immerse yourself in the details of that time. Understand the political, social and cultural context to create an authentic backdrop for your story.

2. **Conduct thorough research:** Research is crucial for historical storytelling. Read books, articles and primary sources related to your chosen time period. Visit museums or historical sites if possible, and consult experts or historians for accurate information.

3. **Select historical characters:** Choose characters that lived during the period you are focusing on. They can be real historical figures or composite characters based on real-life people. Develop their backgrounds, motivations and personalities based on historical context.

4. **Create a central conflict:** Craft a compelling conflict or dilemma that reflects the challenges faced during that historical era. The conflict could be personal, societal or related to significant events of the time.

5. **Blend fact and fiction:** Whilst staying true to historical accuracy, remember that historical fiction allows some creative freedom. Weave fictional elements into

real historical events to enhance the storytelling and engage students. Make sure you highlight the fiction to students when you deliver it.

6. **Use authentic dialogue:** Develop dialogue that reflects the language and speech patterns of the historical period. Avoid using modern phrases or expressions that would not have been used during that time.

7. **Show the historical setting:** Describe the historical setting in detail, including clothing, architecture, transportation and daily life. Transport your readers or audience to that time and place through vivid descriptions.

8. **Include cultural references:** Incorporate elements of art, music, food and traditions from the historical period to enrich your story and give it an authentic feel.

9. **Address historical themes:** Explore themes relevant to the time period, such as power struggles, social injustices, technological advancements or cultural clashes. Use these themes to add depth and meaning to your story.

10. **Focus on human experiences:** Historical stories are an excellent opportunity to highlight the human experience during challenging times. Highlight emotions, relationships and personal growth to make the characters relatable and engaging.

11. **Edit and revise:** After writing your historical story, edit and revise it thoroughly. Check for accuracy, coherence and consistency with the historical context.

12. **Seek feedback:** Share your historical story with others, such as friends, writing groups or historical

experts, and welcome constructive feedback to improve your work.

Finding stories

If creating a narrative may be too time-consuming, find historical fiction books to read from that are as accurate as possible, or find stories within textbooks. You could also try using AI (artificial intelligence) to create a draft story. For example, I inputted this request: 'Create a historical narrative on World War One from one man's perspective.' The story was not perfect and needed checking very carefully. We cannot guarantee that details will be accurate and should do our own fact-checking. However, it gave me something to work from, instead of creating something from scratch.

Remember that historical storytelling requires a delicate balance between creativity and accuracy. By combining well-researched facts with engaging storytelling techniques, you can create historical stories that captivate students and transport them to fascinating periods in the past.

How to deliver the story

Here are some ideas for different approaches to delivering your story.

1. **Set the stage:** Begin by setting the historical context for your story. Provide background information and explain the significance of the events or people you are about to discuss. This helps students understand the broader context in which the story unfolds.

2. **Information cards:** Use information cards to establish a narrative of events without the pressure of having to deliver the story verbally. Enliven the story in whole-class review through your own teacher talk. You could also ask students to interrogate the cards in order to move students from the narrative to the analytical.

3. **Structured role play:** Explore the use of structured role play in parts of the story to keep students engaged; you should play the role of narrator. This works particularly well with KS3 students, who enjoy the opportunity to get actively involved in the lesson.

4. **Visualisation:** Use images to support your narration and help engage students. I did this with my Year 12 students when teaching them about Henry VII's foreign policy using picture notes. See Further reading for an example by Hugh Richards.

5. **Newsroom simulation:** Use a newsroom simulation in which students write a news report for the following day's paper on a dramatic event, such as the Battle of the Little Bighorn, outlining key events and issues using breaking news reports. Students are likely to be actively involved in the task. You as the teacher can narrate the breaking news and ensure pace and challenge by adapting the speed or quantity of information and handling any conflicting information.

6. **Use biographies:** Historians look to individual lives and stories as a way of understanding wider society and processes of change. Using biographies helps to weave little and big stories to create an interplay between overview and depth. (See Rachel Foster's article in Further reading for more on this.)

7. **Incorporate primary sources:** Integrate primary sources, such as diaries, letters, photographs and artefacts, into your storytelling. These authentic materials can help students connect with historical figures and events on a more personal level. Display the sources on your slides and handouts.

8. **Adopt different perspectives:** When narrating historical events, consider presenting the story from different perspectives. This approach encourages critical thinking and helps students understand that history is often complex and open to interpretation.

9. **Create a storytelling atmosphere:** Encourage a relaxed and attentive environment when sharing historical stories. Dim the lights, use props or visuals and speak with enthusiasm to make the experience more immersive. Use body language and vary your tone of voice to create suspense, excitement, sadness, etc. You could, for example, add a fireplace display (from YouTube) to create an atmosphere or add sounds of war/battle if telling stories about war.

10. **Engage with dialogue:** Use dialogue or quotes from historical figures to add depth and authenticity to your storytelling. This can give students insight into the personalities and motivations of key individuals.

11. **Emphasise the human element:** Highlight the human side of history by focusing on individual experiences, triumphs, challenges and emotions. Personal stories resonate with students and make historical events more relatable.

12. **Encourage student participation:** Involve your students in the storytelling process. Ask

open-ended questions, encourage discussions and invite them to share their thoughts and reactions to the stories.

13. **Connect to the present:** Relate historical events to current events or contemporary issues to show students the relevance of studying history. Helping students see the connections between the past and the present enhances their understanding and interest in the subject.

14. **Incorporate multimedia:** Use multimedia resources like images, videos, maps and interactive presentations to complement your storytelling. Multimedia can enhance the visual appeal of historical narratives and provide additional context.

What should students do whilst you are telling the story?

Here are a few ideas.

1. **Comprehension questions:** Identify parts within the story to pause for students to answer comprehension questions.

2. **Storyboard:** Ask students to turn what you are saying into a storyboard.

3. **Accompanying handout:** If you provide students with an accompanying handout to follow, students can highlight key information, e.g. causes in one colour and effects or impact in another colour.

Centre enquiries on stories

Another way to incorporate more stories into your lessons is to centre enquiries (see Chapter 4) on stories. Some great examples of using stories as enquiry questions are given in the Further reading below.

FURTHER READING

- 'Curating the imagined past: world building in the history curriculum' by Michael Hill (2020) discusses the power of storytelling.

- '"Compressing and rendering": using biography to teach big stories' by Rachel Foster (2023).

- 'The surprising story of Henry Tudor' by Hugh Richards.

- 'Telling stories and teaching history' by Hugh Richards (2017).

- 'Jaws and the Peasants' Revolt: what history teachers need to know about storytelling' by Dan Townsend (2020).

- '"The best way for students to remember history is to experience it!" Transforming historical understanding through scripted drama' by Helen Snelson, Ruth Lingard and Kate Brennan (2012).

- '#11 This week, in history… I'm remembering to make my teaching memorable' by Jonathan Grande (2023).

- 'Using individuals' stories to help GCSE students to explain change and causation' by Matthew Fearns-Davies (2021).

Examples of enquiries based on stories:

- Richard Kennett's Cold War enquiry (2023).

- Paula Lobo's World War One enquiry (2020).

- Rachel Foster's early medieval Christendom enquiry (2023).

Summary

- Stories bring history to life and help make knowledge memorable, exciting and nourishing.

- Find or create your own stories, following the steps in this chapter to help ensure they are both compelling and embedded in historical accuracy.

- Explore varied approaches for delivering your stories, make your delivery exciting and engaging, and invite student participation.

- Consider making an enquiry based on stories.

9

Supporting all students

This chapter is written with Laura Tarantini-Amor, EAL (English as an additional language) and SEND (special educational needs and disabilities) consultant for a multi-academy trust.

Inclusive, high-quality teaching responds to the strengths and needs of all students and is about teaching for the success of the whole class. What does this look like in practice for teaching history? How can a teacher plan a lesson for a class of 30 that ensures all students have the opportunity to learn?

Planning for high-quality teaching requires: knowledge about different effective teaching strategies (see the examples in this chapter); knowledge about individual students' learning profiles; and, of course, knowledge of the spread of content and skills from KS2 to KS5 and how they build in your subjects. There are also the mediating factors of environment and presentation. It also involves building relationships with both the learners and their families to figure out what works.

Let us look at some concrete strategies for providing high-quality, inclusive teaching when working with students with learning differences. It is important to note that these strategies are good starting points but there is no guarantee that they will work well for all students all the time. If an approach does not appear to be working for a particular student, teachers need to consider what is not working and how it could be changed. You can find further resources on teaching students with learning differences on the online resource centre.

Labels

Thinking about your class according to 'labels' can be overwhelming (e.g. one child with social, emotional and mental health needs (SEMH), two with dyslexia, one with autism, five students receiving pupil premium). Instead, try to see the diagnostic labels as a starting point for further enquiry that can support your adaptive teaching. Some students will have an education, health and care plan (EHCP) that lists barriers to their learning and recommended teaching strategies and resources. As you find out more about the students in your class, you will find common teaching strategies that you can employ to adapt your teaching so that it responds to the strengths and needs of all. It is important to note that detailed assessment of each individual's needs is essential when trying to establish which approach to adopt when teaching students with learning differences.

Keep your expectations high

If you do not believe a student can do it, why should they believe they could? Do not plan a lesson thinking to yourself that this part of the lesson is only for the 'most able' or 'Jack won't be able to do this' or 'extended writing is too difficult for our students'. Your job is to help them *to be able to* do these things.

Make sure that your curriculum planning and lessons are structured well through using enquiry questions (see Chapter 4) and keep your expectations high to support *all* students to get better at history.

'Five-a-day' campaign

The Education Endowment Foundation (EEF) campaign 'Five-a-day' suggests teaching approaches that have a good evidence base for supporting students with SEND to make good progress. They are helpful approaches for all learners and some of them have already been discussed in detail in earlier chapters of the book. They are:

- explicit instruction
- cognitive and metacognitive strategies
- scaffolding
- flexible grouping
- using technology (Aubin, 2022).

Let us look briefly at each approach.

Explicit instruction

Explicit instruction involves you as the teacher demonstrating in the first instance, then suggesting guided practice, and finally independent practice. A focus on explicit instruction means that students with learning differences can rely on a teacher's expertise during teacher-led lessons. Independent practice may come later on for students with learning differences than it might for other students. Strategies such as 'I do, we do, you do', with steps that involve modelling and constructing together as a whole class, will give all students, including students with learning differences, confidence to complete independent practice. This strategy could be used in activities such as constructing a timeline or looking at a map and working out why battles took place at certain locations. There are further suggestions and ideas for approaches involving explicit instruction throughout the book, particularly in Chapter 6.

Cognitive and metacognitive strategies

Cognitive strategies are strategies or techniques students can use to learn or memorise. For example, you could encourage your students to use a mnemonic to remember certain details.

Metacognitive strategies involve students evaluating their own learning processes. You can provide opportunities for this in your lessons, asking students to think about how they tackled a particular task and whether they could do it differently in the future.

Introducing cognitive and metacognitive strategies can help all students but particularly those who may have trouble, for instance, with working memory, starting a task, sustained attention, planning or time management. These are all skills that serve as the building blocks to even a basic access to history curricula.

You can also minimise the cognitive load so that students can focus on the key learning. If your students have executive functioning impairments and they have to remember where to collect their books from, find the right page, find a pen, remember the date, process multistep instructions and then hold onto those instructions in their working memories whilst performing the task you set them – chances are, they are not learning any history. Perhaps have the book on the desk ready for them or hand them a pen. Keep tasks short and simple, with instructions delivered orally and visually. Use phrases like 'Shall we start this together?' or 'Would you like a sentence starter?' to get them going. Focus on what you want your students to learn whilst in your classroom, and then support their executive skills to help them access that learning.

SUPPORTING SONNY, A HISTORY STUDENT WITH AUTISTIC SPECTRUM CONDITION (ASC), WITH LESSON SEQUENCE IN A SEND CLASSROOM

Sonny was a charming Year 8 student who had significant language processing issues and social communication needs. He was in my SEND history class with 13 other students. Sonny had little sense of sequence, comparison, interpretation or inference. His ability to follow instructions was limited to one information-carrying command word at a time: 'Write the date. Underline the title. Look at the illustration. Now look at the left side of it.' If this was not said to him directly using his name, he did not understand that a class instruction applied to him as well.

ASC was not the only type of SEND in the class. I needed to think about which strategies would help Sonny and hit the needs of some of my other students.

Sonny in particular needed guiding through a lesson sequence so he could keep up. I designed a tick-list approach for him that I put on slides in the lesson and taped to a mini-whiteboard on his desk. I kept the slide and the printout for his desk the same – this meant less for him to interpret. 'Write the date down.' He would do that and tick it off on his list. 'Write the lesson title down.' Again, he would tick it off. I had to think carefully about the lesson structure and the short commands that accompanied it.

Three academic objectives and three learning checks were often too much for the class as a whole, whilst appropriate for some. I therefore planned for a core objective (what was essential for this class to take away from this lesson – often the idea of a sequence or past time frame); a secondary objective (involving facts and a storyline); and a third objective, which involved making connections or inferring motives, and was an extension for those for whom interpretation might be a relative strength.

The next lesson always recapped the previous core and secondary objectives and then focused a bit more on the third objective. I kept this the same for three reasons:

1) Change would throw Sonny and the others into disarray, sending the learning backwards.
2) I could measure what each student could cognitively achieve against my expectations, knowing it was appropriately differentiated.
3) I could sense where and when to push for more progress. (I could also see which topics or concepts were easier or more challenging and feed that back to the history subject lead for actioning.)

Scaffolding

Scaffolding involves providing temporary support for students and then taking it away when the student no longer needs that support. This is something we are likely to do for all our students but we might keep the scaffolds in place for longer for a student with learning differences. Sentence starters, as already mentioned, or structure strips are examples of possible scaffolds that you could use in history. There are example sentence starters later on in this chapter and in Chapter 7.

Flexible grouping

The EEF suggests that students can benefit from working in temporary, flexible groups, including mixed groups of students with a range of different attainment levels. This can provide opportunities for collaborative learning. This approach could also involve temporarily grouping together students who need additional support to help them remember certain details or carry out an activity. Groups should not remain fixed for a long period of time as this can have a negative impact on students' view of themselves. It is important to use formative assessment to make sure that you are completely up to date on a student's learning needs and to help determine what grouping would offer the most support for your students.

Using technology

Students who have difficulty expressing themselves in writing can make use of speech-to-text software, and those who are unable to process dense passages of text can use the text-to-speech function in word processing or other software. Technology can also allow teachers to model worked examples in the classroom (for example, see suggested uses of a visualiser in Chapter 6), and help students to record and reflect on their own learning.

READING STRATEGIES FOR MATT, A HISTORY STUDENT WITH DYSLEXIA

Many students will read an excerpt first and then the questions, but students with dyslexia should be encouraged to read the questions first and then the excerpt, so they do not spend all their energy decoding or trying to see the text (in the case of visual stress), leaving them little energy to formulate an answer. Reading the questions first allows them to search more efficiently for information by using both scanning and deeper reading techniques.

Highlighting the question and the pertinent information found in the text using the same colour helped Matt to reference the information easily when formulating an answer. This stopped Matt from laboriously rereading the text and losing time. He gained marks and began producing Grade 5 answers.

Although Matt had improved, he still did better when listening to information rather than being made to read it. We explored the possibility of providing access arrangements to give him access to a human reader, if he wanted it. However, he preferred using read-aloud technology through the accessibility settings on Microsoft Word™ or a reading pen, as it helped him feel more independent. Because he was cognitively able, he could cope with the robotic tone of the reading pen without that affecting his overall aural comprehension. After practising with it in class, on assessments and at home, he used one for his mock exams and got a Grade 6+.

Factors to consider in your history classroom

Below we discuss different factors to consider so that you can support all of your students in their learning.

Layout and structure

Layout is at the root of many accessibility issues. If you adopt a dyslexia-friendly approach, the vast majority of your learners will be able to read it. Many students have no idea that they have visual stress; they just know they cannot read something easily. A clear structure is likely to help your dyslexic, autistic and attentionally disordered students because it helps them to orient.

IMPROVING SLIDE LAYOUT FOR SCARLETT, A KS3 HISTORY STUDENT WITH LANGUAGE DELAY AND DIFFICULTY IN RECEPTIVE UNDERSTANDING

Although a native English speaker, Scarlett over-applied grammatical rules incorrectly as if she were learning English as an additional language. 'I just *camed* to school' she would explain impatiently if challenged on her lateness to first period. Scarlett was assessed to have an extremely poor working memory and some learning needs. She could not tell a story in sequence and could not give appropriate markers (first, then, next, after, finally) so that a listener could follow her recount of an event.

She had extremely slow processing of spoken language, leading to a large amount of frustration and explosive or avoidant (truanting) behaviour. This meant that by the time you got to the end of a couple of sentences, she had forgotten the beginning! Life was disjointed and inexplicable to her – and school felt like an impossibility.

Scarlett, like many students with SLCN (speech, language and communication needs), could not cope with long teacher exposition. She would become overwhelmed with processing too many words and would walk out of class. Her learning needed to be shown to her and the words added in afterwards. I needed to keep my sentences short and my talk minimal, whilst pointing to a very clearly laid out picture-based slide.

Several points are worth outlining in terms of slide structure:

- Sentences need to be on one line only. I shortened them to ensure they did not cascade onto a second line.
- List key information items as a numbered list, not bullet points. This saves using too much language to explain where the student should be looking on the slide. You want them to be processing the information, not your extraneous directional language.
- Put a box/outline around everything, including pictures, and leave space around each box.
- Put all information into table structures to help students find information quickly.
- Dual coding (see Chapter 6) will help students to interpret the task type and the instructions. Use simple icons or photos, but no fancy clipart, as it is another layer of things to interpret.
- Resist the temptation to explain – point, mime, act out and use minimal language.

Pace and independence

Students who struggle with processing will need a task that stays on the screen. These students will have trouble processing and organising multiple sources of information like separate documents, websites and additional slides to complete a task. That is because it is taking all their working memory to focus their attention, process the letters or the information-carrying words, understand and interpret the layout and structure of the task, or keep the outcome in mind that they are working towards. These students need something simple on screen and maybe one other piece of information to refer to, e.g. a topic mat on their desk.

Other students in your class, however, who can juggle all those bits of information and inputs and independently carry out a task, can be directed to the extra material, independent reading and writing tasks, references to other websites and open-ended questions.

Multimodal engagement

Allow students to experience their learning or show their understanding in different ways. Labelling visuals, drawing Venn diagrams, watching videos, acting answers out, standing up or down if they understand, building things in their rooms, giving them music to listen to whilst interpreting a picture – these all help students access varying strengths and use them in their learning. For interest and maximum engagement, build in a variety of modes across several lessons.

Also note that teachers who are very still when they teach can make it difficult for their students to read them. Move around; use your arms and face. Act things out.

Learning difference and teaching history

In this section, we consider elements that are specific to history teaching and how best to support your students in their learning and skills development.

Facts

Autistic learners can sometimes retain very detailed information about elements such as dates, equipment, troop movements or battles. I once had a student who knew the words to all the most popular songs sung by troops in the trenches during World War One.

Chronology

Conversely, chronology or the ability to hold separate items of information in a sequence may be difficult for students with additional speech and language needs. Often, if the student has an EHCP for a specific language impairment, the ability to sequence events cognitively and then call up the language to talk about them sequentially is difficult for them. That is why most teachers train their students to memorise sentence starters in a structure.

TEACHING SEQUENCE AND TIMING TO SONNY, A HISTORY STUDENT WITH AUTISTIC SPECTRUM CONDITION (ASC), LEARNING IN A SEND CLASSROOM

Another tool I used with Sonny (featured in the case study earlier in this chapter) was a timeline. For Sonny, this needed to be located in 'space', not in time – this means a timeline that I printed (with visuals) and put on the floor for students to walk over. This was more valuable than a small one above the whiteboard with which they could not interact. A small visual timeline meant they had to unpack 'time' and meaning visually and mentally and hold it long enough to apply it to a third cognitive process: understanding the wording of a question about it and structuring an answer. This was quite difficult for their working memories; for Sonny, it was impossible.

Next, I developed a box of props. This might be a laminated portrait picture, a hat with a big plume, an old-fashioned pair of glasses, a maid's bonnet, etc. The combination of standing on a part of the timeline whilst holding or wearing a related item was enough to get Sonny to associate a concrete mental picture with the historical era of the topic.

I would then experiment with the general descriptive language he needed to understand sequence. Comparative language is tricky for literal students. If I say 'old' or 'modern', is that more comprehensible than 'farther away' or 'closer' from us in time? What do I mean by 'modern'? And whose 'modern' do I mean? The Victorians considered themselves very modern and the engineering and architecture of that time very advanced.

'But aren't the Victorians "old", too?' Would 'old, older, oldest' work better?

'Before' and 'after' seem concrete, but in history, they are always relative. To make them concrete, they need to be 'topped and tailed' by years on a timeline. This is where a small amount of descriptive language on cards, a desktop timeline and picture cards can help. Sonny, with support, could put the picture cards along a short timeline and then place descriptive, sequencing words underneath. He could then write short sentences showing understanding of a basic sequence of events. Once that work was done, it might be easier for him to 'get' that someone in the 'oldest' part of the timeline might see things differently to someone in the 'old' section and that the 'old' section was relatively closer to our 'modern' time.

To go through this process, the subject lead and I had to make decisions about which language stipulated by the exam specification could be exemplified and which was too abstract. Thus, we had an ongoing conversation throughout the year as we experimented.

Images

You may think that images will be more accessible for students with learning differences or certain forms of learning difference. However, a student with SLCN or ASC may not understand the inferences in a picture.

If a student has SLCN or ASC, it can be helpful to train them to look at a particular part of the picture, so that they can at least describe some of it. Think about one or two things they might be able to infer from the picture and, in the context of an exam, how they might gain a few marks.

Themes and threads

One key theme in history is that it presumes that students can see a common lateral thread in very different events. The idea that different groups of people in a society at different times in history held different attitudes, often about the same thing, can be challenging for autistic students or those with social communication difficulties. Some autistic learners may have an inability to see things from another person's point of view. Be aware of this and plan accordingly in your teaching.

Learning difference representation in the curriculum

As discussed in Chapter 3, representation is important so that all students can see themselves reflected in your curriculum. Include figures that had learning differences within your curriculum. This will help to affirm our students with learning differences or physical disabilities. The textbook *A New Focus on... British Social History, c. 1920–2000 for KS3 History: Experiences of disability, sexuality, gender and ethnicity* (Snelson et al., 2023) is a great resource to help you ensure representation in your curriculum.

World building

World building in history involves using our imagination to construct visual representations of the past, which is underpinned by rich knowledge of a world that existed a long time ago (see also Claire Sargeant's case study and slide resources on the online resource centre). Creating mental representations of the past helps all learners understand historical texts, especially our students with learning differences. Chris Husbands (1996) argues that students need to study history 'from the inside' in order to see the past as a whole world of experience, which involves the application of the imagination. Storytelling is a powerful example of this (see below).

Storytelling

Storytelling helps students with ASC to master language skills, improve listening skills, increase attention span, develop curiosity and creativity, and better understand non-verbal communication. See Chapter 8 for more detail on storytelling.

Explicit teaching of vocabulary

New terminology should always be pre-taught, so that when students come across new words in a text, the cognitive load is reduced. For more strategies on this, please see Tom Hopkins-Burke's case study in Chapter 10. We should also support students to use the new words themselves. Having encountered the words through pre-teaching and recognised them in a text, the teacher might ask a question that uses that word. Then pupils would be expected to use the word, supported as necessary.

Word banks and knowledge organisers

Word banks and knowledge organisers can be helpful ways to provide information to students with processing issues. See the case study below for a fuller example of this approach in practice.

SUPPORTING SCARLETT, A KS3 HISTORY STUDENT WITH LANGUAGE DELAY AND DIFFICULTY IN RECEPTIVE UNDERSTANDING TO BUILD KNOWLEDGE

I concentrated on small amounts of discrete language associated with images to help her get '100 per cent' on labelling tasks. Once she felt more confident, we could progress to short concrete sentences about the image using the key words. I used the below techniques to build confidence in her topic knowledge.

- Giving small numbers of key words and an image to label helps students to build a basic knowledge of the topic.
- 'Who, what, where, when' questions should be used first.
- 'How and why' questions require a high level of abstract thinking and synthesis of knowledge – often teachers start with those and this leaves the student with SLCN having little chance of success.
- Give the student a set of sentence starters for the types of knowledge you want them to evidence: 'This is a...'; 'This happened in...'; 'This means that...'; 'I agree because...'; 'I disagree because...'

Scarlett could not mentally call up any semantic webs when given a concept. This meant that she could not look at a portrait and think 'rich', 'privileged', 'well-fed', 'educated', 'powerful', 'manor house', 'servants'. Students who can do that would have a pre-existing semantic web built around understanding daily life and a 'rich' or 'poor' version of it.

If I wanted Scarlett to infer or offer related terms, i.e. 'rich' equals 'wealthy, privileged and powerful', I needed to give those to her in a way she could access. A simple way to do this is a sorting activity, where words on cards or in a word bank could be categorised under 'rich' or 'poor'. That would then give Scarlett some handy vocabulary to describe what was needed and ease her working memory, which was unable to call to mind related words.

Knowledge organisers are useful for students with milder processing issues. They can look over the information and remind themselves of the missing piece. Scarlett would be unable to access so many words in one place; it would overwhelm her processing. However, an empty visual organiser, wherein she puts the words into simple relational groups, is perfect because it economises her processing capacity to focus on the task at hand.

Retrieval tasks

Many students with learning differences benefit from a focused review of previous content, which is helpful for all students. Most of my lessons have a retrieval task as a 'Do now' or starter task (see Chapter 10). This acts as a 'daily review', which is the first of Rosenshine's ten principles of instruction (Rosenshine, 2012). A focus on recall and building it into the curriculum design will ensure that the things students learned previously are activated more frequently. This means the loop between the working memory and long-term memory is activated with every review.

Adaptive teaching

On a more general note, adaptive teaching is a very helpful approach to take with all students, including those with learning differences. This involves continually assessing the strengths and needs of learners and adapting your teaching accordingly. In practice, this could be circulating and noticing things in books and then doing something about it. Related to this, we discuss feedback in detail in Chapter 7.

Summary

- Plan for high-quality teaching that is responsive to the strengths and needs of all students.

- Everything we do to improve the attainment of students with learning differences should also improve the attainment of all students.

- Have high expectations of all your students. Remember that if you do not believe in your students, it can be hard for them to believe in themselves.

- Integrate the approaches from the 'Five-a-day' campaign into your teaching: explicit instruction, cognitive and metacognitive strategies, scaffolding, flexible grouping and use of technology.

- Consider layout and structure of materials, pace and independence and multimodal engagement when planning lessons.

- Bear in mind how different students may respond differently to particular aspects of history, such as chronology, themes, vocabulary and so on, and consider strategies to support them.

- Continually assess the strengths and needs of your learners and adapt your teaching accordingly.

10

What makes a great history lesson?

Over the last few chapters, we have considered key strategies for the history classroom, including: developing knowledge and skills, retrieval practice, modelling, metacognition, reading and comprehension, writing skills, feedback, storytelling and supporting all students. In this chapter, we bring these elements together into the context of a lesson structure.

Planning a strong history lesson is a bit like baking a cake. You invariably need the key ingredients of strong subject knowledge, positive relationships with your students and an understanding of effective pedagogy, but you can adapt elements of the recipe or the cooking method as needed. Your students are your chief tasters and they all have different dietary requirements and appetites for learning. Let's face it, some of them do not even want cake, but it is up to you to use your 'teacher magic' to make it academically nutritious and enticing.

This chapter will look at a possible structure for your history lessons and further ideas for specialist 'ingredients' you might want to include within it.

Structuring your history lesson

The lesson structure shown in Figure 10.1 below is the one our team follow when planning to ensure meaningful learning is occurring. We will use this as the structure for our chapter as we go through the different elements.

Start
- Retrieval starters
- Reminder of big picture
- Key word(s)

Setting the context
- Source or interpretation work
- Video or teacher explanation

Distilling of new knowledge
- Main task
- Progress check

Application
- Exam practice or paragraph writing (extended writing)

Plenary
- Enquiry planning sheet
- Key takeaways
- Conclusion

FIGURE 10.1: *Example lesson structure*

Retrieval starters

Retrieval starters are a brilliant way of getting the lesson off to a strong and focused start by encouraging your students to make links between previous and upcoming learning. Sometimes, these connections need to be made explicitly so that students understand the purpose of the lesson and understand how the lesson fits into the broader scheme of learning. Retrieval starters can be knowledge- or skills-based and can link to learning from the previous week, term or year.

Revisiting key content in knowledge-based retrieval starters embeds the knowledge in the minds of the students and enables them to progress further in their learning.

Skills-based starters could be visual or written hooks into the new learning, such as constructing arguments or source or interpretation analysis. This encourages students to apply their skills to new contexts and builds confidence. Name the skill and make it explicit so students are aware of what they are practising and can see the progress they are making.

For example:

- When teaching about William the Conqueror, ask students to write down three things they know about the role of rulers or monarchs from previous learning, including from primary school.

- Before teaching the formation of the Metropolitan Police, complete a low-stakes knowledge quiz on medieval justice.

- As an introduction to Elizabeth I, use the *Armada Portrait* and ask students to evaluate whether Elizabeth is shown in a positive or negative light and why.

- When introducing a lesson on the Bristol Bus Boycott of 1963, ask students to make a judgement about the level of equality in the UK now and explain their thinking.

The big picture

Continually reminding students of the 'big picture' (our enquiry, see Chapter 4) is one way to help students connect new knowledge to existing knowledge rather than seeing each piece of knowledge as separate. Every lesson we remind students of the big picture within our particular enquiry at the start and plenary of the lesson. In addition, after each enquiry, students come back to the overarching enquiry question for the year by completing an activity within their homework booklet. Therefore, students are constantly revisiting knowledge, whilst the overarching enquiry helps students to see the connections and relationships between various enquiries.

Introducing key words

In order for students to have a meaningful understanding of new key words, it is important that they create a mental model of the word. We can teach this not just by using a dictionary definition but also by using Frayer models or accompanying the key word with images in order to build a connection between students' prior knowledge and the new key words.

Tom's case study below delves into ways in which we can teach new key words and develop literacy.

VOCABULARY IN THE HISTORY CLASSROOM

Tom Hopkins Burke, history and politics teacher and Literacy Co-ordinator at an academy in Nottinghamshire, @HB_History

SEEC: a model of explicit vocabulary instruction

As literacy leader in my school, I introduced Alex Quigley's SEEC model (Quigley, 2018):

- **Select** the vocabulary to be taught.
- **Explain** the meaning of the vocabulary.
- **Explore** the deeper meaning of the vocabulary.
- **Consolidate** through retrieval practice, homework and application to writing.

(From *Closing the Vocabulary Gap* ©2018 Alex Quigley, page 140, reproduced with permission of the Licensor through PLSclear.)

Selecting new vocabulary

Quigley (2018) suggests a variety of questions regarding which words should be selected at different stages of the curriculum. As a history teacher, I find it most helpful to think about his prompts on the words that children are unlikely to know already, which appear frequently and which are most necessary in order to understand a text.

Explaining new vocabulary

It can be tempting to ask students what they already know about a word; however, there will be some students who bring misconceptions to the table that then may be picked up by other students. Therefore, it is important that we prioritise telling students what words mean, rather than asking them what they think a word might mean. This means that all students will leave your lesson with the same understanding and meaning, minimising the reach of any misconceptions.

Quigley (2018) suggests both saying and writing words as a class. This focus on sound (phonology) and spelling (orthography) is important to eliminate common misconceptions and boost confidence.

Once students have practised saying and writing the word, the next step is to provide a student-friendly definition. This is not the same as a dictionary definition; it is important to make this as accessible as possible. A common approach is to use a Frayer model, a type of graphic organiser. Figure 10.2 gives an example Frayer model for the word 'fascism'.

Curriculum sequencing is important here. Students who have learned about the rise of communism will be able to explain why fascism (which emphasises the authority of the dictator or ruling elite) is different to communism (which proposes a classless society). Students without this prior knowledge will need instruction on the differences between fascism and communism.

Exploring new vocabulary

At this stage, a teacher might perform a check for understanding and move on with the lesson. However, through exploring vocabulary, students can understand new words in depth.

Two of the most useful strategies to build vocabulary depth are etymology (the history of a word) and morphology (how words are formed).

Etymology

Teaching the etymology of a word helps to deepen students' historical understanding. For example, the word 'fascism' is derived from the Italian word 'fascio',

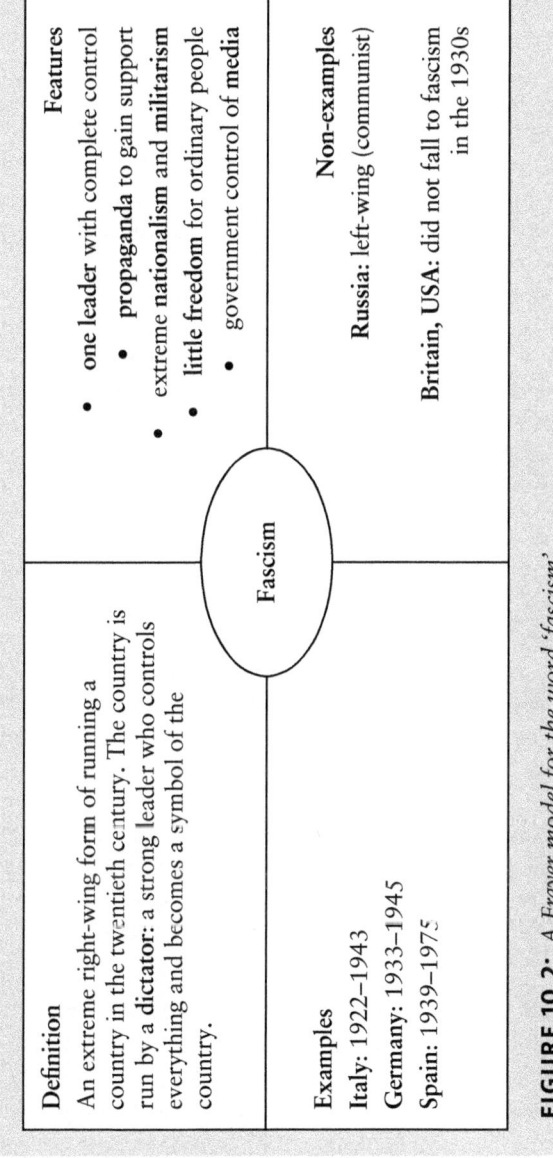

Definition

An extreme right-wing form of running a country in the twentieth century. The country is run by a **dictator**: a strong leader who controls everything and becomes a symbol of the country.

Examples

Italy: 1922–1943
Germany: 1933–1945
Spain: 1939–1975

Fascism

Features

- **one leader with complete control**
  - **propaganda** to gain support
- extreme **nationalism** and **militarism**
- **little freedom** for ordinary people
  - government control of media

Non-examples

Russia: left-wing (communist)

Britain, USA: did not fall to fascism in the 1930s

FIGURE 10.2: *A Frayer model for the word 'fascism'*

meaning 'bundle', and it was used to refer to a bundle of rods tied around an axe in ancient Rome, symbolising unity and strength. Understanding the origin of the word 'fascism' helps students to understand the name of Mussolini's National Fascist Party and to understand why the first fascist movements of the twentieth century arose in Italy. This builds students' sense of chronology as they study the rise of fascism.

Students who are confused about the words 'parliament' and 'government' can be taught that 'parliament' comes from the French word *parler*, meaning 'to speak', whereas government is derived from the Latin word *gubernare*, meaning 'to steer' or 'to pilot' a ship. So, whilst a parliament discusses the issues of the day, a government controls the country.

Morphology

Words can be broken down into different parts: root words and affixes (prefixes and suffixes).

History teachers can benefit from teaching particular affixes and root words explicitly. If students know the meaning of a particular affix or root word, they can learn more words. For example, 'democracy' can be broken down into the root word 'demo' (from the Greek word *demos* meaning people) and the suffix '-cracy' (from the Greek word *kratia* meaning power). Therefore, democracy can be understood as 'power by the people'.

From this knowledge, students can understand more words with the suffix '-cracy':

- Auto**cracy**: power by one person (*auto* = 'self')
- Pluto**cracy**: power by the wealthy (*pluto* = 'wealth')
- Aristo**cracy**: power by the ruling class (*aristo* = 'best')
- Theo**cracy**: power by religious authorities (*theo* = 'god')

In addition, students can understand more words with the root word 'demo':

- **Demo**graphic: characteristics of a particular group of people (*graph* = 'writing' or 'representation')
- Pan**dem**ic: a disease affecting people across a large area (*pan* = 'across')
- **Dem**agogue: a leader who appeals to people (*agogos* = 'leader')

Root words and affixes can be considered a 'cheat code' in explicit vocabulary instruction, as a way of allowing students to understand the meaning of multiple words in one go, saving teaching time across a curriculum.

Consolidating new vocabulary

If learning is to be considered a change in long-term memory (Kirschner et al., 2006), explaining and exploring a new word in one lesson does not mean that students have learned that word. As part of consolidating vocabulary, retrieval practice ensures that the new vocabulary is recalled from memory, strengthening the learning process. This could be as simple as recalling words based on definitions, or vice versa.

Another task could be to spot where a word is not being used correctly, testing students' understanding of vocabulary in context.

Perhaps the best form of consolidation in history is when students complete essays or extended writing. As part of our assessment, we can check to see how well students can use the vocabulary we have taught explicitly, and whether there remain any misconceptions. This can be used to refine the teaching process for future cohorts.

Setting the context

Before teaching new content, we often present students with a source and ask thems to tell us what they can learn from the source about a particular topic. This encourages students to think hard and reminds them that historians learn through sources. It is also a great way to integrate more sources into lessons. You will find more suggestions for working with sources throughout the book.

Main task

When creating lessons, coming up with activity ideas can sometimes be difficult. At times like this, we can draw upon research. Research that heavily informs my ideas for main tasks comes from Fiorella and Mayer's book *Learning as a Generative Activity: Eight Learning Strategies that Promote Understanding* (2015).

Generative learning considers the learning experience from the point of view of the learner. In this approach, we ask what students should do with the information that they have been given to ensure that they are able to truly make sense of it and learn it in a way that allows them to apply it to a new situation.

In my own practice, I commonly use the following activities that promote generative learning:

- summarising
- mapping
- drawing
- imagining. (Fiorella and Mayer, 2015)

What do these strategies look like in teaching history?

Summarising

Definition: Restate the main ideas of a lesson in one's own words.

Benefits:

- Involves selecting key information – this is a skill that students need to have in history as they should be able to select relevant evidence, facts or quotes to be able to support their claims.

- Creates deep learning – as it forces students to think hard about what they are reading, extract the key information, make links and associations within new material and then make associations with material they already know.

- Has been shown to increase retention and learning – as it requires students to attend to both the higher meaning of the material and the gist of it (Craik and Lockhart, 1972; Bretzing and Kulhavy, 1979).

Examples:

- Carry out guided reading.

- Students summarise each paragraph into a sentence – this helps us to see whether students understand the gist of the text. You can differentiate by providing students with statements that summarise each paragraph of content and ask them to match the statement to the paragraph.

- Provide limited space for notes so that students do not simply copy the information/textbook. This forces students to think carefully about the important content and the types of words they are using.

- When looking at the significance of individuals, e.g. activists of the civil rights movement, give students the template of an outline of a person for them to annotate with each person's actions and impact.

- If you have a high-achieving class, you can ask students to swap books so that they are making summary notes for somebody else. This adds a sense of duty to ensure that summary notes are properly done.

- Model good practice for note-taking and summarising text.

- Give students statements from which they find and add content from each paragraph to support the statements.

- Mind maps help students construct meaning from a text. Begin by breaking the text down into a series of headings, e.g. What happened? Why? Impact? Or Who? What? Why? Where? When?

Mapping

Definition: Connect a text into a diagram or graphic organiser. Benefits:

- Helps students to organise what might seem like distinct, separate knowledge into a more coherent or united form.

Examples:

- Create a flow chart for cause and consequence.

- Create a visual flow diagram of the chronological events in a particular time period, e.g. the Battle of the Little Bighorn. This activity is great for building students' understanding of the narrative of a particular event.

- Create a Venn diagram to show change and continuity.

- Students create a mind map of all they remember about a particular topic, and then use a different colour to link together the knowledge they remember.

- Create a relationship web of factors.

You can find a case study about 'world building' and mapping from Claire Sargeant, along with example resources, on the online resource centre.

Drawing

Definition: Transform a text into a visual form.
   Benefits:

- If drawing is used, it is far more likely that a learner will engage with the information.

- Students cannot directly copy text in this approach, encouraging them to engage deeply with the text.

- Transforming the text into visual form also takes advantage of dual coding (see Chapter 6).

Examples:

- Picture notes – this is when the pictures are combined with mapping to show the relationships between the various images.

- Storyboards.

Imagining

Definition: Form internal images to illustrate the content of a lesson.

In this strategy, ask learners to create mental images of their learning from verbal or written information. You can provide prompts and ideas as needed. It is important to note that the quality of materials used to help students imagining is vital.

Benefits:

- Just as with mapping and drawing, we are providing students with the direct opportunity to create links in their learning.

- The links to prior learning in this process are significant.

Examples:

- Write a narrative account using sources or artefacts to help. If you want to make this task more challenging, ask students to write in the style of a particular historiography, e.g. revisionist or traditional historian.

- Write a historical fiction novel.

- Design a children's storybook.

- Design a museum exhibition.

- Create a Trip Advisor review about a period in history.

- Write a script for a narrator of a documentary or *History Today* podcast about a period/event in history.

- Create a storyboard.

- Create a play or drama piece on a particular event (choosing your event carefully and sensitively; see Chapter 3).

- Create a diary using the sources and textbook to help.

Further useful approaches for the main task

Below are some other useful approaches and strategies to consider when planning your main task. These are:

- chunking

- support and challenge

- modelling

- practice opportunities

- worksheets

- talk

Chunking

Chunking is a way of grouping information into smaller components to enhance learning. This enables you to introduce new content or skills precisely to avoid misconceptions and over-generalisation. Teach content in sufficient depth so that students to have a good understanding of the subject and avoid superficial knowledge.

Chunking the lesson allows you to keep the lesson running at a good pace, and learners are less likely to become disengaged. It also reduces the risk of cognitive overload as information is introduced slowly. Chunking allows you to break down a task into building blocks to gradually raise your students up to success; more blocks can be added across the key stage as your students progress.

For example:

- When teaching source analysis skills, start by asking students to annotate three to five features they see in the source. Check for understanding before then introducing inferences or utility. For source analysis, there are various popular acronyms to break down content, provenance, purpose, audience, author and other components to support students, and these individual elements could be chunked as they are introduced.

- Present subject-specific vocabulary and then ensure students have a chance to use it later on in the lesson (see the case study later on in this chapter for further ideas).

Support and challenge

The content of what is being taught should be consistent across classes and teachers. However, how that content is presented will vary depending on the needs of the students in the room. Groupings like students receiving pupil premium (PP), high prior-attaining students (HPA) and students with EAL have their benefits but can sometimes become a homogenous blur, so it can be beneficial, for both you and your students, to look over the resources and activities through a particular student's eyes. This is similar to making good use of the support plans for students with learning differences. When planning, instead of reflecting on how this lesson could generically work for traditional groupings, pause and think about how this lesson would look for an individual student in your room. You could also use this opportunity to ensure that your curriculum is as inclusive and representative as it should be and make sure there are not entire societal groups forgotten or misrepresented (see Chapter 3). Historical skills are invaluable in the world we live in so, regardless of whether a KS3 student opts to take the subject at GCSE, for example, every lesson should be academically rigorous and accessible so that all students can reach their full potential (see also Chapter 9).

For example:

- Students who lack confidence could benefit from sentence starters, structure strips or other forms of support that can then be gradually reduced as their confidence grows.

- Ask students to complete five to ten low-stakes knowledge questions and conduct whole-class feedback before doing a written assessment relevant to the first activity. This is a quick win to build self-belief in reluctant learners and give them a positive start.

- Encourage all students to 'speak like a historian' and present their ideas orally. This can be especially useful for students who find written work challenging.

- Provide 'aiming higher' or 'challenge' tasks at every opportunity but make it very clear that all students can attempt them. There are no ceilings to your expectations of your learners. These tasks might require higher-level skills such as evaluation or applying their learning to a different context.

- If a student is interested in a particular topic, recommend wider reading, listening or watching to further develop their skills and build those habits of success as early as possible. Some students may even have suggestions for you as well.

Modelling

Modelling the skills, knowledge and behaviours you wish to see in your students is invaluable (see Chapter 6). This can be done using model paragraphs, visualisers or just by thinking carefully about how you speak within the lesson. When practising particular skills, encourage students to think like a historian and lead the way in showing them how to act like one too.

Ultimately, knowledge and skills are not the only factors you will be modelling. Your classroom is your kingdom and you control the climate for learning. If you are modelling high expectations in terms of effort, behaviour and focus, the students will follow. If you have low standards, so will they.

For example:

- When practising an assessment question, model your thinking in approaching it.

- Give students a model paragraph and ask them to underline elements like subject-specific vocabulary, using evidence, making a judgement, explanations or evaluations. Go through this with them and pick the paragraph apart.

- Give students a paragraph and ask them to identify and fix any errors or make improvements.

- Practise what you preach. Make sure you speak and write like a historian and empower students to correct you if you do not.

Practice opportunities

In order for students to really build confidence and hone their skills, they need to put them into practice. If you are familiar with the 'I do, we do, you do' method of structuring lessons (see Chapter 9), this is the 'you do' and is arguably the most important in terms of embedding learning. Ideally, every lesson should include a practice opportunity for at least one skill, whether that is constructing an argument, analysing evidence or evaluating causes or effects of a particular historical event or figure. The only way to become truly proficient in anything is to 'practise, practise, practise'.

For example:

- If you have just modelled tackling an assessment question, students could attempt a similar question independently.

- Students lacking in confidence could benefit from sticking with the same activity you have just modelled. For example, show them one side of the argument and then ask them to write the opposing side.

- Give students an extract of a historian's work. This is ideal for practising interpretation skills as the task allows students the opportunity to 'read like a historian' and pick apart the information or viewpoint.

- If you are tight on time, ask students to plan an answer rather than writing it. That way, they are at least putting those planning skills into practice.

Worksheets

You can read a further case study on using worksheets to set meaningful activities from Andy Hassan on the online resource centre.

Talk

Although I prefer students to complete the main task in silence, it is important to use talk techniques when it is appropriate for the learning task. To avoid talk leading to distraction, it is vital that students understand the importance of their discussion, and teachers must provide children with the language tools and scaffolding they need to think and learn though talk.

Progress check

You can check for understanding throughout the lesson, and many of the strategies suggested here can be used at any point. Having a segment of the lesson designated for progress checks can help to ensure consistency within the department, though.

The progress check segment of my lesson involves students testing themselves on previous learning. It could take different forms, such as:

- Students write down everything they remember from the introductory phase of the lesson and main activity on a whiteboard from memory (brain dump activity).

- Students create a concept map from memory based on what was just taught to them.

- Display short-answer quizzes on the board for students to answer on their whiteboards from memory. The key is to select the core knowledge you would like students to retain from the main activity and introductory phase of the lesson.

Checking for understanding is only meaningful if it enables teachers to identify and fix gaps and misconceptions in students' understanding. There are many ways to do this, such as using multiple-choice questions or hinge questions. Designing effective multiple-choice or hinge questions takes time, so plan this work in advance.

Questioning needs to go beyond surface learning and genuinely assess whether students have fully grasped a concept or are just parroting words or phrases you have taught them without any deeper understanding. If a student is incorrect, only includes basic details or does not answer like a historian, a wonderful mentor once advised me to use the phrase 'go again' to give them the opportunity to change or add to their response.

Regularly using formative assessment techniques, such as questioning, or total participation techniques, like mini whiteboards, is only useful if it leads to a change in your practice moving forward. When assessing, it may be that your students have nailed it and can move on, but it may also require some reteaching, which is OK – learning is not a linear process.

For example:

- Use multiple-choice questions where all of the answers seem like they could be viable at first glance. This is an ideal method of checking for misconceptions.

- Total participation techniques like coloured cards or mini whiteboards enable you to check the understanding of all of your learners quickly and provide instant feedback as the correct answers are revealed.

- Avoid only using basic knowledge-based questions like dates and 'name one feature of...' and create opportunities for students to practise higher-level skills, such as explanation and evaluation.

- Do not just take the student's first answer and move on. Use phrases such as 'go on' or 'what else could you add to that?' to encourage them to deepen their thinking.

Alex Gordon's case study below gives many other ideas for ways to check for understanding.

APPROACHES FOR CHECKING WHOLE-CLASS UNDERSTANDING

Alex Gordon, history teacher and Assistant Head of Sixth Form

The use of mini whiteboards is one strategy to check for whole-class understanding (see my thoughts on this later on in the case study), but there are a range of further approaches that I use in my lessons.

When using these strategies, it is vitally important that the teacher acts on the information received and 'does' something with this in the moment to drive the learning forward. We are consistently making judgements as to whether the learning can proceed, any scaffolding can be removed or we need to reteach anything.

To check for understanding effectively, it is suggested that language such as 'what have you understood?', as opposed to 'have you understood?', is most effective as students are asked to articulate a response. It is important that a classroom environment is established where mistakes are encouraged and risks taken. This will show us – as the teachers – more and allow us to work out any errors and misconceptions that may need to be retaught.

Hand-number voting to answer a question

Ask the class a question and instruct them to present their answer with their fingers. This may only work for short or numerical-based questions. You could also use this approach if asking a multiple-choice question and students are voting for a particular answer.

Thumb-voting to answer a question

Ask students to display a thumbs up or thumbs down to answer a question.

Heads down and eyes closed number voting

Ask students to close their eyes or place their heads on the desk and vote using their fingers.

This ensures that students cannot look at their peers and potentially copy any answers.

Using colours, letters or numbers to vote and answer a question

Students write down a letter or number or show a colour to vote for a particular answer.

Hands up and cold calling

When you ask a question, all students raise their hands to show their attention and understanding. This creates a culture of enthusiasm and a love for learning. The teacher then scans the room and strategically selects a student. This also supports the creation of a classroom culture where 'I want to get picked and be asked to contribute'. (This is also a strategy to check for listening or attention.)

Choral response or chanting

Ask all students to chant the answer to a question. The teacher can listen for any errors or misconceptions due to the answers given or the volume of the responses.

Think/pair/share or turn and talk

Ask students to discuss an idea or a question with their partner prior to the whole-class discussion. This should be kept short and sharp to ensure the discussions are focused. This can build student confidence when giving an answer to the class.

Using mini whiteboards

In my view, mini whiteboards (MWBs) are the single most effective resource we possess in the classroom, and they should play an integral role in our practice. Personally, I can no longer imagine a history lesson where MWBs are not on student desks and used consistently.

MWBs allow teachers to assess not only the understanding and learning of their students at any given moment in the lesson but also the prerequisite knowledge prior to teaching new content. Principally, they enable the teacher to be active and enterprising in gaining information from all students in order to make a decision about whether the lesson needs to be adapted or whether they can progress with the next stage of learning. This can be achieved because the use of a MWB signals a clear expectation to students that *all* need to participate and that there is no opt-out in the lesson. Through the information gained as a snapshot of the students' understanding, the teacher will have a solid appreciation of which knowledge areas or questions need to be retaught or repeated in the future through retrieval or in the main body of the next lesson.

In our history classrooms, MWBs are not just for short-answer or factual-based questions. They can be used in a variety of different ways:

- longer-answer questions
- essay planning
- practice essay writing
- prompts for debates
- drawing or annotating a story or process from the past.

Through the questions posed and the routines established, students are given adequate thinking time to write their answers. The transient and short nature of the tasks mean students are less likely to worry about mistakes because any errors are easily erasable and it is easy for teachers to live mark and assess the progress of their students in the moment.

It can sometimes be argued that MWBs are too much effort to use and it is a waste of lesson time to organise the handing out and cleaning up process. There is also, sometimes, an apprehension that students will doodle and use them incorrectly, especially in classrooms where there are potential behaviour issues. Therefore, for MWBs to be used effectively and smoothly, students need to be aware of *why* the teacher is using them and the routine the teacher or the school uses in lessons with MWBs.

The progress check phase shows me how well students have retained information within the lesson. Of course, successful recall does not mean that new knowledge has landed well in their long-term memories. Therefore, future lessons should feature the same or similar questions as a 'do now' retrieval task.

Furthermore, just because students can recall information, it does not mean that they understand the new knowledge. Therefore, the application segment of my lessons are very important to check for understanding (see below).

Application

In this phase of learning, students need to apply their new knowledge to a source question, exam question or lesson title question. In history, we need students to have a good understanding of key facts, but we also need them to be able to use that information in a fluid and flexible way.

Application of knowledge in some form of an extended answer allows students to connect their knowledge, achieve fluency and consolidate knowledge in their long-term memory so that they can recall and use the knowledge easily.

Example strategies:

- Elaboration – ask further questions such as: When? Where? Why? What? Who? (the five Ws) and How? This makes students expand their answers and show their understanding. An example would be to place a picture of the topic/event (e.g. the Reichstag 'Night of Long Knives') and place the five Ws as question stems around the picture for students to answer on their whiteboards.

- Give your students short sentences linked to the topic and ask them to elaborate on that sentence, extending the initial point further using their own subject knowledge from memory. In essence, the task is to 'finish off my sentences from memory'.

Plenary

It is good to check student understanding at the end of the lesson to help plan next steps. This might be done through, for example, questioning, responses on MWBs, using red or green cards to indicate understanding or exit tickets. The plenary may even take the form of a written response, e.g. a paragraph, conclusion to the big question within the lesson title, quiz or longer written essay.

The aim of a plenary is to gather feedback from students that can be used to inform the next lesson. If a large proportion of the class seem not to understand, then you may need to reteach content the following lesson. Alternatively, if the majority of students have displayed understanding, then the next lesson can consolidate learning and move students on.

Examples:

- In KS3, my students are required to answer the enquiry question or complete an enquiry planning sheet. This helps students to see how each lesson fits into the enquiry.

- In KS4, my students tend to do an application task or another retrieval task.

- Sometimes I ask students to summarise their learning into five bullet points and draw an image or diagram next to each point.

- Sometimes I use the plenary segment to leave students in suspense so that they look forward to the next lesson.

You can find further, specific examples of ways to support students at KS4 and KS5 on the online resource centre, including case studies from Jen Brown, Sally Burnham and Rebecca Chadwick.

Refining your 'recipe'

The 'ingredient list' in this chapter is not exhaustive and there are a plethora of other ideas and methods out there. There are also entire books that focus on the individual elements mentioned. Just like baking a cake, your lessons inevitably will not always go to plan. Sometimes the recipe does not work so needs adapting or scrapping completely. Through gaining personal experience and observing and engaging with other practitioners, your skills will flourish and your bakes will improve. So, keep mixing your ingredients together with a sprinkle of your 'teacher magic' and watch your young learners rise to the challenge. Before you know it, planning a successful KS3 lesson will be a piece of cake.

Summary

- Planning a strong history lesson requires strong subject knowledge, positive relationships with your students and an understanding of effective pedagogy.

- A shared lesson plan model within your department can ensure meaningful learning takes place consistently.

- An example lesson structure might include: retrieval starters, a reminder of the big picture or enquiry, key words, source work, explanation, main task, progress check, application and plenary.

- Effective elements of a main task might include: chunking, support and challenge, modelling and practice opportunities.

PART 3

Developing yourself

11

Owning your own CPD

Research suggests that improving student outcomes happens, at least in part, due to improving yourself as a teacher. 'Having a very effective, rather than an average, teacher raises each pupil's attainment by a third of a GCSE grade.' (The Sutton Trust, 2011, p. 5)

We expect our students to do reading or extra work beyond the lessons, and so we should too. CPD should not be limited to twilights or INSET sessions; it should be an ongoing process throughout our career. We can take leadership and ownership of our professional development, knowing our own strengths and weaknesses.

There is a belief that some teachers are better than others, or that some are born to teach. I would argue that this is not true. During my PGCE, my explanations lacked clarity and coherence because I was timid and shy. I was so nervous I used to stutter. Tasks I would set in lessons were not compatible with the knowledge students needed to retain. My first set of A level and GCSE results were not good. However, I was committed to improving my practice, and cared about both my students and my craft of teaching.

I set myself yearly goals to improve my practice as a teacher. I have found that taking ownership of my own CPD has been both empowering and enjoyable. This has also increased my confidence and wellbeing and has led to career progression (from KS3 lead to KS4 lead, lead practitioner, specialist leader of education (SLE) and then head of department).

This chapter explores ways that you can take ownership of your CPD and improve your practice.

Observations

Being observed by others

We know that our students improve when we offer them feedback. In the same way, it is important that we get feedback from others. Observations can cause anxiety and fear for some teachers, but they can really help us to develop. It can be very useful to get a fresh pair of eyes to offer feedback and especially to help us recognise our blind spots.

Observing others within your school and department

Observing others within your department or outside is great for seeing modelled best practices. This year, one of my targets was to improve my explanations. I was able to observe my colleague, whose explanations are a particular strength. She is a second-year ECT, yet as head of department, I was able to learn a lot from her. Through observing her, I was able to see how she pitched and animated her voice and used imagery to illuminate her explanations.

Find out the strengths of everyone in your department and visit those who have the qualities you wish to improve upon in your own practice. For example, when I was an ECT, I would observe a more experienced teacher every Friday in period 1 to hone my subject knowledge and see how she taught exam skills to Year 11.

Observing others outside your context

By using social media, I have been able to connect to other schools to observe best practices in other contexts. This year I asked a local school whether I could come in and see what teaching and learning is like in their history department. The head of department kindly agreed, and it was great to see best practices in terms of offering feedback after an assessment, teacher explanations and collaboration at work. This improved my practice as both a head of department and a teacher.

Last year, a teacher from a different local school reached out to me to visit my department and focus on teaching history A level, as his school would be introducing A level next academic year. He was able to see how we teach A level and the differences from teaching KS4. Through looking at students' folders and work booklets, he was also able to see the level of work expected at A level. This gave him confidence and insight into teaching A level classes.

Social media

X (formerly Twitter)

Through X, I have gained ideas and been introduced to history conferences and books. This platform is great for gaining support and inspiration, especially if you work in a small department. It allows you to connect and interact with educators outside your school and area. The history teacher community on X is a great staffroom to be in and I am grateful for the growth and opportunities it has given me. Please do not let the negativity that can sometimes occur put you off, and remember that you can ignore, mute, block or report if needed.

When sharing or finding resources, you can use hashtags such as #HistoryTeacher, #EdexcelHistory, #AlevelHistory, #AQAhistory or #OCRHistory. If you are sharing resources, hashtags help you to widen your audience beyond your followers; if you are trying to find resources, hashtags can help with the search.

If you want to have curricular conversations, you can hold 'X spaces'. Alternatively, you can listen in if you do not want to host. This is a great way to express your views, ideas or experiences, whilst connecting with other educators. It is fun to discuss history education with other passionate educators in a friendly and informal online environment. Be brave: why not start your own history 'spaces' on a weekly or monthly basis? You can invite historians to the platform to discuss a specific period/event or you could discuss various historical concepts.

Facebook

There are many Facebook groups offering advice and sharing resources. I have used these groups to ask questions, network and share resources. Often these groups have a Google drive where resources are shared and you can upload your own resources. It can be great to see how others plan or teach in various contexts; it leads to inspiration and can save starting from scratch. I have also used these groups to take pictures of work and get advice on feedback or marking.

Here are some Facebook groups you might find useful:

- KS3 History

- New AQA GCSE History 2016

- Edexcel GCSE History Teachers support group

- IBDP History Teachers: Support Group

- OCR A level History support group for teachers

- Teachers of AQA A level History

- OCR SHP GCSE History advice group

- Edexcel GCSE History

- Edexcel A level History teacher support group

- Cambridge (CIE) IGCSE History Teachers: Support Group.

There are many more. Try typing what you are looking for into the Facebook group search.

You can also join local history groups. Some teachers teach outside of their local area, so their knowledge of the school's local history may not be strong. You can use local history groups on Facebook to develop your knowledge and get some pictures, or even get a speaker to come in to speak about their local experience of World War Two, growing up in the 1960s, etc.

LinkedIn

LinkedIn is a large professional network where users can set up an account that is essentially an online CV. It is great to connect with others in your field and a good way to read different educational articles. Like X, it also provides a good way to keep up with current affairs, latest updates, trends, research and debates surrounding history education. It is also useful for recruitment purposes and sharing your ideas.

Audiobooks and podcasts

Audiobooks and podcasts are great forms of professional development as they can offer CPD on the move. You can listen to audiobooks and podcasts whilst cooking, getting yourself ready for school, driving or at the gym. Chloe Oliver, who contributes a case study below, points out that podcasts can be great for interesting anecdotes and can be masterclasses in storytelling. I personally enjoy Dan Snow's *History Hit* podcast, the *History Hotline* by Deanna Lyncook and *Versus History* by Dr Elliott L. Watson, Patrick O'Shaughnessy and Conal Smith.

Reading

Chloe's case study below discusses how reading has improved her teaching practice. She gives suggestions as to what to read, especially if you have to teach a period of history you are not confident in. As history teachers, there are always periods that we are more adept in than others. However, reading short books, as Chloe's case study mentions, can be a great way to fill in the gaps.

DEVELOPING YOUR SUBJECT KNOWLEDGE THROUGH READING

Chloe Oliver, second-year ECT, @ChloeOHistory

Working to enhance your subject knowledge will make you more confident in the classroom and, over time, will give you that effortless quality of experienced history teachers who teem with good stories and knowledge. You can draw a great deal from books, podcasts and documentaries, which can be consumed little and often.

Short bursts on a commute into work or during a leisurely walk over time build up to a great deal of new knowledge. Short books, like the Oxford *Very Short Introductions* and the Penguin *Monarchs* series, and their bibliographies, are a great starting point for an intelligent overview of a subject area.

If you do not have access to it already, find out whether your department has a subscription to the Historical Association, along with a print subscription of its journal *Teaching History*. If not, invest in one. *Teaching History* is the place to find the latest research and wisdom from fellow history teachers. Its regular features on key debates in history, outlines of fundamentals of history teaching and advice on how to move on in your practice are invaluable. Engaging with *Teaching History* will help you to become well-versed in the common understandings and vocabulary of the history teaching community. This will help you in many respects, including being able to engage more meaningfully with the wider community and to think more deeply about teaching history itself. Rereading *Teaching History* articles year after year has benefitted me in my first years of teaching as, with each reading, I have been able to bring to them greater layers of knowledge from my time in the classroom.

The long history and culture of *Teaching History* itself has generated many reading lists and bibliographies, of which Michael Fordham's *Guided Bibliography for History Education* (2015) is one of the most comprehensive.

Professional communities

Subject associations like the Historical Association are at the heart of teacher and curriculum development. I believe that every history department should subscribe to the association and their articles can be discussed in departmental meetings. The Schools History Project is another valuable resource for support, information and development.

Various other communities to learn from include the History Teacher Book Club (@historybookgrp) and Be Bold History Network (@BeBoldHistory). The Be Bold History Network holds webinars with academics to help teachers improve subject knowledge and use of scholarship in lessons, whilst the history book group helps get teachers reading current historical books and holds discussion events with the authors. Both networks are great in terms of developing teacher subject knowledge.

University history departments

University history departments are often eager to work with schools and may run events or other CPD. See whether there is an outreach team or schools liaison contact whom you can speak to in the first instance.

Conferences

There are many subject-specific conferences that you can attend, such as the HA Conference (organised by the Historical Association) and the SHP Conference (School's History Project). During these conferences you learn so much and are able to network and make friends for life. I often leave feeling inspired and refreshed. I would also encourage you to present at the events, which can in turn lead to other opportunities.

Blogging

Blogging is a great way to share ideas, but it can also help you to reflect on your own practice and learn from others through their blogs. Blogs that have helped me to progress include:

- Historical Association 'One Big History Department': https://onebighistorydepartment.com

- Paula Lobo: https://lobworth.com

- Jonathan Grande: curricularpasts.wordpress.com

- Jonathan Mountstevens: https://occamshairdryer. wordpress.com

- Simon Beale: https://historyiseverystory.wordpress.com

- Mike Hill: https://intheoldendays.home.blog

- Hannah Cusworth: www.hannahcusworthhistory.com

- Alex Benger: https://monsieurbenger.home.blog

- Joshua Vallance: https://mrvallanceteach.wordpress. com

- Greg Thornton: https://mrthorntonteach.com

- Kristian Shanks: https://kristian-shanks.medium.com

Examining

Becoming an A level examiner helped me to understand exam technique better. I was able to see how to get students from a B to an A and from an A to A*. I was able to glean best structures from students' responses and then teach it to the following cohort.

After gaining understanding through exam marking, I then began to plan and write many exam questions. I realised that if I did not know how to write a grade 9 essay or A* essay then I would not be able to teach that process to my students. This then gave me the confidence to live model my thinking processes in lessons. I in essence became a student in order to teach.

Summary

- Improving outcomes for your students comes, at least in part, from improving yourself as a teacher.

- You can take ownership of your CPD through observing others and being observed, making contacts and sharing ideas using social media and other professional communities, attending conferences and examining.

- Improving your subject and pedagogical knowledge and finding out about new research gives you fresh insights and enthusiasm.

- We always tell students that they are responsible for their own learning; likewise, we are responsible for our own development.

12

Head of department and other roles

In this chapter, we consider what the head of department role looks like and other roles you might like to consider as you develop in your career.

Head of department role

Heads of history are required to advocate for their subject within school and ensure that senior leadership are kept up to date on matters such as specification changes and the role of history in contributing to literacy. Heads of history also provide the inspiration, support and guidance that colleagues need in order to teach history well and develop their own careers. To the students, the head of department represents the subject and conveys their own passion and hard work to act as models for young learners.

There are many facets to this role and it is not always easy, but I hope that the guide in this chapter will help to give you a good sense of the role and what it entails.

Strategic direction

The head of department sets the strategic direction for their team. They start by defining a clear vision for the department that aligns with the overall goals of their school, and they determine the department's mission statement, long-term objectives and key performance indicators. Successful departments will have clear goals: they need to know what they are for and why. Once you start with the 'why', the 'how' and 'what' become easier. A shared vision is vital for a department's success. It becomes the filter through which we decide whether to adopt or refuse new initiatives. The vision helps us to keep focus (see Chapter 1).

Decision-making

As a middle leader, the head of department will be making decisions every day. When it comes to making good decisions, I find Andy Buck's STOP model (Buck, 2018) helpful. This is an acronym for: Situation, Temptations, Options, Plan. Check that you have understood the situation fully; ensure that your decision will not be biased or based on an emotional response; consider your options; and make a plan.

Leading teacher development

As discussed in Chapter 11, subject-specific professional knowledge is important and makes a difference to student outcomes.

When creating a programme of CPD for your department, the programme should be informed by results from public exams and targets from your various monitoring systems, like book looks, data and learning walks, etc. Your CPD curriculum for your department should be responsive to the needs of the staff.

Your department could focus on one to three targets of improvement for an academic year. Targets could include:

- improving students' extended writing

- improving fluency of reading

- improving students' oracy

- improving teacher explanation

- improving the teaching of evidential thinking

- improving the teaching of causation.

Whatever your overarching target(s) will be for the year, break the target down into granular steps to develop in various departmental CPD sessions or meetings. The idea is to build incremental improvement throughout the year.

Figure 12.1 shows an example of working with one target throughout the year.

Leading quality assurance

Quality assurance generally involves using a mix of approaches, including lesson observations, book looks, data and student voice, to monitor and improve the provision within your department.

Lesson observations (learning walks)

I use a template for this to record my thoughts on various aspects. The form helps me to see strong and weak areas within the department and inform training for the team. You can find an example template on the online resource centre.

Developmental focus for the year: improving students' extended writing	
Session	Focus
1	Teaching students how to make strong points or claims
2	Explicitly teaching students how to select relevant evidence to support claims (evidential thinking)
3	Explicitly teaching students how to select relevant quotes from sources or interpretations to support or challenge claims
4	Improving our live modelling to help students develop their explanations
5	What does a strong conclusion look like?
6	What does a strong and concise introduction look like?
7	Teaching students how to sustain their argument
8	Providing effective feedback for improving historical writing
9	Teaching students how to plan
10	Moving from describing the past to explaining the past
11	What does a good causation essay look like? Approaches to effective teaching
12	What does a good significance essay look like? Approaches to effective teaching

Developmental focus for the year: improving students' extended writing	
13	What does a good change and continuity essay look like? Approaches to effective teaching
14	Approaches to teaching how to write a narrative question (GCSE)
15	Approaches to teaching how to write a consequence question (GCSE)
16	Approaches to teaching how to write an importance question (GCSE)
17	Approaches to teaching how to write a 'How far do you agree…?' question (GCSE)
18	Approaches to teaching how to write an 'Explain why…' question (GCSE)
19	Approaches to teaching how to write a 'How useful…?' question (GCSE)
20	Approaches to teaching interpretation questions (GCSE)
21	Approaches to teaching AO1 essay questions (A level)
22	Approaches to teaching A02 essay questions (A level)
23	Approaches to teaching A03 essay questions (A level)

FIGURE 12.1: *Developmental focus for the year: improving students' extended writing*

Book looks

In our department meetings, we devote 15 to 20 minutes to looking at a set of books for a particular year group. I request staff bring to the meeting an example of a book from a student with learning differences, a student receiving pupil premium and a student at a particular grade. Then, in pairs, we discuss the quality of the work using the structure of 'what went well' (WWW) and 'even better if' (EBI). You can find an example template for this on the online resource centre. Although targets are provided, when feeding back to the whole department we focus on sharing good practice to avoid embarrassing staff.

Data

Data helps us to know how well our students are progressing. As head of department, you also need to provide your team with the data that will help them reflect on what is working and what is not, and respond accordingly. Question-level analysis can be a powerful tool to raise standards. If, for example, you see a particular teacher's class performing exceptionally well in eight-mark questions in comparison to the rest of the team, then ask that teacher to lead CPD on how they maximise outcomes for the eight-mark question. In any given area, is there a skill or content area in which students underperform in a particular class or in all classes? Is there a subject knowledge gap within teaching that needs to be addressed? Do boys perform better or worse than girls in a particular area or question? All staff should be clear about their role in providing accurate and timely data and planning effective interventions. Use data to celebrate success for both staff and students as well.

Student voice

I have found student voice to be most effective when I interview students with their books alongside them. *Pupil Book Study* by Alex Bedford has helped to transform my approach to student voice (Bedford, 2021). Looking at books in isolation may not reliably tell you how well students engage, participate and remember the taught content. However, talking with learners and studying work in their books at the same time can be powerful.

Figure 12.2 shows an example timetable to follow when completing 'student voice book studies'.

I try to ensure that an interview has no more than six participants and it typically takes between 40 minutes and an hour. I generally ask five or six questions. This approach

Half term	Students to be interviewed
HT 1	KS4 students with learning differences
HT 2	KS3 students with learning differences
HT 3	A level students receiving pupil premium
HT 4	Year 11 students performing three grades or more below their target grade
HT 5	High-ability KS3 students
HT 6	1. Year 10 students performing three grades or more below their target grade 2. Year 12 students performing three grades or more below their target grade

FIGURE 12.2: *Student voice book study example timetable*

provides a window into the lived experience of students and a mirror to reflect professional practice. The outcomes of the meeting help to inform departmental priorities and CPD.

Here are some example questions that you can use with students at these meetings:

1. Can you find a piece of work that you are really proud of and tell me why?

2. I can see that you are learning about X. Tell me a little more about this period.

3. Is there anything that has particularly interested you about your current unit or learning enquiry?

4. Explain how we know about the past.

5. Can you show me a quiz you have taken during this study that has helped you?

6. What things in this area of learning really stick in your memory and why?

7. If you were to teach your family something from this enquiry/unit, what would it be? Why?

8. (KS3) The big question for the year is X. What can you tell me so far that can answer this big question?

9. What are your strengths and weaknesses in history and how could you improve?

10. What new word in history have you learned? How have you applied that word?

11. How does what you have learned recently connect with previous knowledge?

12. What do you find most challenging and why? Can you find me an example?

13. How does your teacher support you and help you to learn?

BECOMING A HEAD OF DEPARTMENT

Laura Gladwin, Head of Humanities, Bristol

Learning from others

Ever since my initial ECT year, I have taken on projects within the department to develop my skills outside of the classroom. Having decided during my PGCE that I wanted to become head of department (and later a senior leader) rather than a pastoral lead, I always sought to learn from my head of department, observing what he was doing in his role that I did not yet know how to do. Initially, this involved leading on planning for KS3 schemes of work, then later taking on quality assurance of KS4 assessments. Continually asking questions, learning from those more experienced and therefore gaining experience myself through additional projects all helped me gain proficiency in leadership. We also had several non-specialists teaching history, so I began to lead on supporting them; I helped them with history-specific teaching and they helped me with general pedagogy and teaching practice. By the time the head of department role came up, I had a plethora of projects to talk about and, most importantly, I could show the *impact* that they had had already on our students. My determination to learn and to progress was evident to those appointing.

Experience versus time

The number of years you have been teaching is relevant; there is no doubt about that. However, I think that the word 'experience' relates to two things: how long you have been doing something, but also *what you do during that time*. Whilst I had not been teaching long, I had been sure to fill those years with a range of different experiences. In some ways, this cannot match having done the job for more years, but it did give me more insight than others might have with the same number of years' experience.

Clear vision

Have a clear vision for what you want to achieve. You must know what your vision for your department is, so that you know what you want to achieve with them. This must be a clear vision, shared (and possibly developed) with the team. The emphasis here is on the word 'with'; you must work with your team and bring them on the department development journey with you; otherwise working together may become fraught. This vision should also link to the school's vision. When applying for head of department jobs, research what the current department and school visions are. Whilst you want to have your own aspects of the vision, it is not advisable to change the department's aims entirely.

Finally, your vision may also include your own professional development, regarding how you intend to grow as a leader.

Final advice

Develop a good awareness of your knowledge and skills, in terms of what you both can and cannot do so far. This will allow you to address any gaps in your experience and help you to become a well-rounded leader and teacher. Read literature, speak to those already in middle leadership roles and listen to the wisdom of those you trust.

AN OVERVIEW OF BEING HEAD OF DEPARTMENT

Swerupa Gosrani, Head of History

Administrative tasks

Of all the aspects of the role, administrative tasks are perhaps the most mundane, but they are crucial and it is unlikely that anyone else will want to do them. The kinds of tasks that I see as administrative include: ensuring that the correct exam entries are made; making mock exam papers; sharing mark schemes; ordering stationery; setting appropriate cover when people are away; booking visits and filling in all the appropriate paperwork; and also checking and ordering communal resources. This can include cleaning out cupboards, throwing away old resources and updating communal display boards. I would also see filling in any documents that SLT (senior leadership team) need and analysing data as part of the administrative work. The only time I really analyse data is after exam results. At this point, I look at which papers and questions we did well on and which we need to improve on, and then use this information as a focus for teaching and learning discussions.

Curriculum

Curriculum is probably the most interesting aspect of the role and the reason why many people will go for the job. This involves the strategic thinking about how you want to shape your department and subject, what your rationale is for curriculum content, what schemes of work you should have and what they should include, as well as designing lessons and resourcing them. It also requires thinking about assessment: what type of assessments to have and what the purpose of your assessments will be.

Managing people

Probably the most difficult part of the job is leading your colleagues – making sure you get the best out of them and that they are happy doing the job. This can involve thinking carefully about what classes will be allocated to which individual, so that it is seen as fair and as equal as possible. For example, you might try to ensure that ECTs do not get groups that may be considered 'challenging', so that they can gain confidence, and ensure that any challenging groups are spread around the department.

When looking at GCSE groups, I look at the data, particularly at effort, aptitude and genders of the various groups. I also talk to learning support about the needs of individuals and to the head of year before I allocate groups. I may also need to consider reducing the different number of year groups an individual teaches, so that their planning workload is reduced.

Another aspect involved in leading colleagues is leading on teaching and learning. I have very experienced colleagues, so I have found the best way to do this is through discussion and sharing ideas about how to teach topics or aspects that we may be finding difficult. I explain the rationale for doing things in a certain way, listen and change things if they are not working for everyone. For newer colleagues this can involve letting them watch you or other colleagues teach aspects that they find difficult, or you watching them and offering constructive advice.

I have found that the best way to ensure the wellbeing of your colleagues is to trust them – trust that they will manage their time and get what they need done when it needs to be done. If you find that the trust has broken down, then this is when it may be worth getting advice, either from your SLT or from HR (human resources), about how to deal with this.

Good luck!

BRINGING ABOUT CHANGE AS A HEAD OF DEPARTMENT

Martyn Bajkowski, Head of History in Lancashire

Being a middle leader is one of the most rewarding and challenging roles in school. I have often heard it said that being a middle leader is like being the jam in a sandwich: squeezed by both the teachers within your department and the senior leaders above you. I do not necessarily agree with this analogy. Yes, there is pressure from both aspects, but pressure is in the nature of every role in a school building and there are definitely ways to operate that reduce pressure.

For me, the best analogy to think about as a middle leader is that you are a captain of a ship within a fleet. You are given autonomy and responsibility to navigate the waters ahead of your department. You can spot waves on the horizon and your role is to steer the ship whilst moving forward. That last part is important. You have to move forward as a department. The skill of a middle leader is to know that moving forward means your boat is going to rock from side to side more. Too much change and your boat will capsize, and too little and you will be blown backwards or into the current.

So, for me, success as a middle leader is in plotting a route that supports your staff to do their roles without anything else weighing them down, so that if and when currents do turn, they have the energy to help get your department and themselves back on course.

Anyway, enough of analogies and onto some real examples of how you can bring about change as a head of department.

Consider the capacity within the team to make change happen successfully

History teachers typically have very detailed and specific knowledge about a particular area of history and hardly any knowledge (bar their own learning as an 11- to 14-year-old) about other topics. Finding out about a particular area of history can be a huge barrier to change. Teachers may feel unsure about what students need to know from each activity and lesson and they will not be able to teach and deliver content as well as they can for familiar topics, due to the cognitive load of having to 'think' and 'remember' history as they are teaching it. Therefore, it is crucial to ensure that staff have good subject knowledge of any new topics or new ways of delivering similar topics; otherwise, your change will not happen successfully.

The other thing to consider with capacity is not just their subject knowledge but also their personal and professional situation outside of your department. If they do not have capacity to engage in this crucial subject knowledge acquisition, then it is your job to create such capacity for them.

Presenting a change to the department

When presenting a change to your department, own the decision and meet any difficult conversation head on. I have experienced situations at other schools where middle leaders tell their departments that they are changing their curriculum due to Ofsted or because SLT want them to. The leaders tried to pass the decision to people above their pay grade so as not to lose friends or with a shrugging acceptance of 'What can we do?'. The two things I would say about this is that firstly, people respect and respond to honesty; secondly, they know that you have to make a decision – that is your job.

However, I do think it is important that you involve your team in any decision you make. Whilst you make the final call, and you should own this, you want your department to teach their curriculum – to live it just like you do – and for this to happen, you cannot create it in isolation. It has to be collaborative to be successful. When decisions are made, you make them and you should be honest about your reasons for doing so. Ultimately, the only reason that makes sense is that this is the best thing for the students you teach.

What is necessary?

As a new middle leader, I thought my job was to implement the decisions of my SLT without question. As I have gained more experience, I have fought my department's corner more. The key thing to remember is that you both have the same goal in mind: to deliver the best lessons to your students. Your relationship with SLT is important. Talk about the capacity of your department, ask for support and ask for their rationale for the speed of change. There is a lot to mention about managing upwards, letting them know how and why you want to do something, but the best advice that has worked for me is to be proactive generally. Hit and meet your deadlines early when possible (it makes extensions when you need them easier to obtain), and do not say no straight away. Instead, ask for time to think about how the matter or request could apply to history and then come back with an answer and a logical rationale. You want to have a positive outlook, but you are trying to balance the speed of change so that you can take your department with you.

Focus on one thing at a time

Focus on one thing at a time. If you feel the need to address the teaching of causation, make everything about that: every CPD, every drop-in and every book look. Talk about it in the corridors, after school and in classrooms. Those changes will then become embedded. If you try to change too much in classroom practice too early, it will mean delivery is very varied across the department.

Developing staff

To be successful at developing your staff, you need to understand them as people: their background, family, personal situation, professional experience and goals. Your job is similar to the one you have with your students; you need to understand their strengths, areas that need development and what steps they need to take to develop as a teacher. Unlike a student, however, there is no exam. This allows you to nurture and grow them as they develop as practitioners.

Having helped to develop two ECTs who are now heads of department, I think the most valuable advice is that you need to treat staff as individuals. Each has their own path and their own vision, and your job is to ensure that they are open to development, but you are choosing what development they have in order to support them in that. You can model being open to opportunities and development. Show your interest in internal and external CPD. Lead by example by taking on additional roles to develop yourself.

Be positive

My final piece of advice is to be positive. It is sometimes easy in a school setting to be negative and to complain, when actually this is the best job in the whole world and every leader is trying to ensure the best for their students. So, be positive. Look after your staff so they can do their job and if you give them the right developmental opportunities, they will thrive.

You can find further inspiring and supportive case studies on the online resource centre. These include:

- becoming a head of department from Sophie Hudson

- succeeding as a head of department from Jema Kinsman

- succeeding as a second in history from Rosie Culkin-Smith

- and two case studies on leading primary history from Lindsey Rawes and Fiona Gambles.

Other roles

There comes a point in your career when you think, 'What is next?' You may be at the stage where you are seeking a new challenge. For some, the natural step is to become head of department or part of SLT. For others, they know they want to progress but SLT has no appeal for them. Sometimes doing educational freelance work or other activities can develop your skills. For example, some might consider:

- textbook writing

- authoring articles (whether academic or for educational magazines) or books

- examining

- presenting at a history CPD event

- mentoring

- creating a website or blog, podcasting or sharing resources

- becoming a governor

- completing an MA in history education.

You do not need a senior leadership role to be fulfilled as a teacher. There are plenty of opportunities that can support professional progression and provide valuable experiences, skills and knowledge. A professional challenge can help you to feel you are progressing as a person and educator.

The next few case studies provide brief insights into other roles within school that you might like to consider.

SUCCEEDING AS A HUMANITIES HEAD OF DEPARTMENT

Laura Gladwin, Head of Humanities, Bristol

There is a notable difference between being a head of department for one subject and a head of department for multiple subjects. Some heads of humanities have heads of each subject within their team, but my school does not. Instead, I have one deputy head of humanities, with whom I share the workload.

One of the balances that needs to be made is how work will be distributed between the leaders within your team, ensuring fairness and opportunity for all. Additionally, it must be fair how much time and energy is spent on each subject. For example, as a history specialist, it could be tempting to spend more time developing history schemes of work than those for geography or religious studies. However, it might actually be more beneficial to spend time on the subjects that you are less familiar with, in order to learn the exam specifications and nuances of those subjects. This is even more important if you are not teaching the subject, as you still need to have a working understanding of it to properly quality-assure it.

Additionally, you may need to consider how many students are impacted by the care and attention you pay to each subject. If far more students study geography, more effort may need to go into this than the other subjects. It is important to consider what the priorities are for your department, and who within your department can assist you with achieving these priorities.

Knowing your team

Take the time to get to know your colleagues, both professionally and (where appropriate) personally. I always endeavour, where possible, to visit each of my team once per day, either in their classroom, in the staffroom or by heading to their duty spot. This gives them opportunity to raise anything they need to with me and – I hope – makes them feel supported. Additionally, always making sure to follow up on actions, no matter how small, helps colleagues feel listened to and respected, even if the follow-up is just to say that I am still working on the issue. Investing effort and energy into your team will in turn help them do the same for their students, and create a productive and enjoyable working environment.

ADVICE FOR POTENTIAL SENIOR LEADERS

Kristian Shanks, Assistant Principal for Teaching and Learning at a school in Bradford, @HistoryKss and http:// kristian-shanks.medium.com

Every individual is different, and some teachers are ready for senior leadership at an earlier stage of their careers than others. Some will make significant progress in their role in the same school, perhaps rising from classroom teacher all the way to senior leadership, whilst other people will be itinerant and work in different schools. I think whichever you are, it is important to have the following skills under your belt before becoming a senior leader:

1. Success in your own classroom

Ultimately, as a senior leader, you will be viewed differently by colleagues, even in very friendly and supportive environments. In order for people to place their trust in you, they will want to know you have some track record of success, whether it be as a teacher and/or as a middle leader.

2. Evidence of adaptability

As a senior leader, you cannot wall yourself off into your own remit. You have to be prepared to get stuck in across a range of issues. In my role as lead for teaching and learning, I have had to dive into literacy, SEND, data and behaviour to varying degrees. It may be that at some point my headteacher decides to move me off my current remit to a new area. That is the life of a senior leader, so the more opportunities you have to build a range of knowledge before getting to that position, the better.

3. People management skills

As a head of history, you potentially already have quite extensive experience of people management, perhaps managing both eager ECTs and highly experienced veteran teachers with multiple decades of service. Remember, as SLT you may also have to line-manage people in your organisation who are not teachers. This could include managing non-teaching pastoral managers if you take on a behaviour-type role, an exams officer if you are responsible for data and assessment, or the school librarian if literacy falls under your remit. This can present different issues and challenges that you might not have encountered before. However, the ability to listen, to see things from the other person's perspective and following through on your commitments will stand you in good stead no matter what.

Senior leadership is an incredibly demanding but rewarding role. There is no harm in waiting for the right time and role, and it always pays to do your homework about specific roles.

LEADING HISTORY IN A MULTI-ACADEMY TRUST (MAT)

Kyle Graham, Assistant Headteacher for Teaching and Learning, previously Director of History for the Co-op Academies Trust

I found leading history in a MAT to be one of the best roles within education. It is incredibly unique and fulfilling to have the opportunity to remain in your subject for a prolonged period of time whilst progressing in terms of leadership. However, this role is one that varies massively in terms of both demands and responsibilities from trust to trust.

Curriculum development

Curricula vary massively across different trusts, with some using standardised resources, plans and schemes, and others not. Within my trust, we believed providing a standardised curriculum was not the way forward for us. This meant that there was a lot of work to do in terms of reviewing the resources and plans in various schools and then providing support and guidance on what the next steps were.

Some of the main focus points for me within the time that I did this role were:

- increasing the academic rigour of resources used
- diversification of the curriculum and moving away from an overly Anglo-centric, White male narrative
- increased use of scholarship within the classroom.

The way that I achieved this was by providing feedback to individual departments, leaders and SLT, but also by showing them the resources and research that supported the suggestions I was making. This was particularly key in ensuring that staff could make the changes they required, but also in ensuring that any future changes were made with the full understanding around them.

CPD for staff and leaders

In my role, I was expected to host half-termly network meetings for secondary heads of department, and termly meetings for primary leaders. This was one opportunity to cover subject-specific CPD and share good practice. I would also provide training and CPD for individual departments or individuals within departments, depending upon the need of the school, although that was usually limited to the two or three schools I was in for placements in that year. I also provided training and coaching to staff who were aspiring history leaders.

Subject reviews

Subject reviews took place every other year, and I ensured that a subject review was not the first time I visited a school. The subject review takes the format of a deep dive, but with the express purpose of being as supportive and informative as possible. These were to ensure that everybody knew the current position each department was in, as well as next steps that were bespoke to each school. For me, it would involve:

- pre-visit review of curriculum material and data
- meeting headteacher/SLT link to discuss school/department context
- curriculum meeting with head of department, similar to Ofsted style
- walkthroughs of lessons, with head of department where possible
- book look

- student panel/voice
- feedback to subject leader and SLT link/headteacher.

Improving outcomes

Ultimately, we are judged by our ability to improve the results that our students get. This is the most delicate part of the job, as people are naturally very defensive when it comes to data. For me, it was about finding out where the gaps and strengths were and sharing good practice across the trust.

These are the things that I found most improved the results in our trust.

- Improving quality assurance – getting heads of department to do more regular walkthroughs, book looks, curriculum reviews, standardisation of marking and student voice, in order to find out what training/guidance the department and individuals within it needed.
- Improving lessons – this is obvious, but if the sequencing and rigour of lessons were not right, then the outcomes would not be. It was all about ensuring staff had high expectations of what students could achieve and that they ensured they were emphasising the most important parts of the curriculum at KS4.
- Retrieval and knowledge focus – ensuring that all departments and classrooms were using regular retrieval and were thinking about how their students retained and recalled information was key. It placed a greater focus on staff to know what they wanted students to recall and know over time, as well as within lessons.
- Use of department time – ensuring that it was being used to improve the department as a whole as well as individuals was critical. If we spent too much time on admin tasks, then we were not maximising this. How

did heads of department identify the needs of the department (see point 1)? How did they deliver this? How did they check that their CPD was having the effect they wanted it to?

Ultimately, I found this to be a fantastic role, and one that I would recommend to anybody. I certainly found that I took much away from it. Being able to utilise research across a range of different contexts and with different people is a great leadership challenge and one that will really allow you to hone your skills within your subject and beyond.

Summary

- This chapter has explored key attributes you will need in order to take on a more senior role as your career progresses.

- We have explored the various aspects of the head of department role and considered other roles that you might want to consider.

- Various teachers have shared their own experiences in the case studies to provide first-hand insights as you consider your next steps.

- If middle or senior management is not for you, there are many other possible ways to develop your career.

References

Arthur, J. and Phillips, R. (eds) (2000), *Issues in History Teaching*. Abingdon, Oxon: Routledge.

Atherton, A. (2021), 'Defining excellence: how I use whole class feedback', *Codexterous*, https://codexterous.home. blog/2021/07/15/defining-excellence-how-i-use-whole-class-feedback/#more-1365

Atkinson, H., Bardgett, S., Budd, A., Finn, M., Kissane, C., Qureshi, S., Saha, J., Siblon, J. and Sivasundaram, S. (2018), 'Race, ethnicity and equality in UK history: a report and resource for change', The Royal Historical Society, https://royalhistsoc.org/racereport

Aubin, G. (2022), 'EEF blog: "Five-a-day" to improve SEND outcomes', Education Endowment Foundation, https://educationendowmentfoundation.org.uk/news/eef-blog-five-a-day-to-improve-send-outcomes

Bajkowski, M. (2023), 'Assessment at KS3 in history', One Big History Department, Historical Association, https://onebighistorydepartment.com/2023/07/03/assessment-at-ks3-in-history

Bedford, A. (2021), *Pupil Book Study: An Evidence-Informed Guide to Help Quality Assure the Curriculum*. Woodbridge, Suffolk: John Catt Educational.

Boxer, A. (2022), 'To make sure your students are ready to practise, use mini-whiteboards', *Tips for Teachers*, https://tipsforteachers.co.uk/mini-whiteboards

Bradshaw, M. (2009), 'Drilling down: how one history department is working towards progression in pupils' thinking about diversity across Years 7, 8 and 9'. *Teaching History*, 135, 4–12.

Bretzing, B. H. and Kulhavy, R. W. (1979), 'Notetaking and depth of processing'. *Contemporary Educational Psychology*, 4, (2), 145–53.

Buck, A. (2018), *Leadership Matters 3.0: How Leaders at all Levels Can Create Great Schools*. Woodbridge, Suffolk: John Catt Educational.

Burnham, S. (2007), 'Getting Year 7 to set their own questions about the Islamic Empire, 600–1600'. *Teaching History*, 128, 11–16.

Carr, E. H. (2018), *What is History?* London: Penguin Classics.

Caviglioli, O. and Goodwin, D. (2021), *Organise Ideas: Thinking by Hand, Extending the Mind*. Woodbridge, Suffolk: John Catt Educational.

Collin, J. and Quigley, A. (2021), 'Teacher feedback to improve pupil learning: guidance report', Education Endowment Foundation, https://d2tic4wvo1iusb.cloudfront.net/production/eef-guidance-reports/feedback/Teacher_Feedback_to_Improve_Pupil_Learning.pdf?v=1703911323

Counsell, C. (2004), 'Looking though a Josephine-Butler shaped window: focusing pupils' thinking on historical significance'. *Teaching History*, 114, 30–6.

Craik, F. I. M. and Lockhart, F. (1972), 'Levels of processing: A framework for memory research'. *Journal of Verbal Learning and Verbal Behavior*, 11, 671–84.

Cusworth, H. (2021), 'Putting Black into the Union Jack: weaving Black history into the Year 7 to 9 curriculum'. *Teaching History*, 183, 20–6.

Dawson, I. (n.d.), 'The nature and significance of enquiry in history teaching', *ThinkingHistory.co.uk*, www.thinkinghistory.co.uk/EnquirySkill/downloads/EnquiryCoreArticle.pdf

Department for Education (DfE) (2013), 'National Curriculum in England: history programmes of study', www.gov.uk/government/publications/national-curriculum-in-england-history-programmes-of-study/national-curriculum-in-england-history-programmes-of-study

Fearns-Davies, M. (2021), 'Using individuals' stories to help GCSE students to explain change and causation', Historical Association, www.history.org.uk/secondary/resource/10056/using-individuals-stories-to-help-gcse-students-t

Fiorella, L. and Mayer, R. (2015), *Learning as a Generative Activity: Eight Learning Strategies that Promote Understanding*. Cambridge: Cambridge University Press.

Folorunsho, E., Henderson, S. and Oladehin, T. (2022), *Black British History KS3 Teacher Resource Pack*. London: Collins.

Fordham, M. (ed.) (2015), *Guided Bibliography for History Education*, https://clioetcetera.files.wordpress.com/2016/12/guided-bibliography-history-education.pdf

Foster, R. (2023), '"Compressing and rendering": using biography to teach big stories', Historical Association, www.history.org.uk/secondary/resource/10638/compressing-and-rendering-using-biography-to-te

Frankopan, P. (2016), *The Silk Roads: A New History of the World*. London: Bloomsbury Publishing.

Graham, K. (2023), 'The power of enquiry questions', in A. Fairlamb and R. Ball (eds), *What is History Teaching, Now?* London: John Catt, pp. 129–34.

Grande, J. (2023), '#11 this week, in history… I'm remembering to make my teaching memorable', *Curricular Pasts*, https://curricularpasts.wordpress.com/2023/02/19/11-this-week-in-history-im-remembering-to-make-my-teaching-memorable

Griffin, E. (2013), *Liberty's Dawn: A People's History of the Industrial Revolution*. New Haven, Connecticut: Yale University Press.

Harris, H., Burn, K. and Woolley, M. (2013), *The Guided Reader to Teaching and Learning History*. Abingdon, Oxon: Routledge.

Hill, M. (2020), 'Curating the imagined past: world building in the history curriculum'. *Teaching History,* 180, 10–20.

Husbands, C. (1996), *What is History Teaching? Language, Ideas and Meaning in Learning about the Past*. London: Open University Press.

Kennett, R. (2023), Tweet, 28 February 2023, @richkbristol, https://twitter.com/richkbristol/status/1630548160480198656?s=20

Kirschner, P. A., Sweller, J. and Clark, R. E. (2006), 'Why minimal guidance during instruction does not work: an analysis of the failure of constructivist, discovery, problem-based, experiential, and inquiry-based teaching'. Educational Psychologist, 41, (2), 75–86.

Lee, P. and Ashby, R. (2000), 'Progression in historical understanding and teaching approaches among students ages 7–14', in P. Stearns, P. Seixas, and S. Wineburg (eds), *Knowing Teaching & Learning History: National and International Perspectives*. New York: New York University Press, pp. 199–222.

Lee, P. and Shemilt, D. (2003), 'A scaffold, not a cage: progression and progression models in history'. *Teaching History*, 113, 13–23.

Lobo, P. (2020), 'What do the stories of the "often forgotten armies" reveal about the Western Front?', *Lobworth*, https://lobworth.com/2020/05/14/what-do-the-stories-of-the-often-forgotten-armies-reveal-about-the-western-front

Maraschin, J. (2020), 'Reflections of a White teacher in a multiracial, post-apartheid classroom, *Miss Folorunsho*, www.missfolorunsho.com/2020/07/reflections-of-white-teacher-in.html

Nuthall, G. (2007), *The Hidden Lives of Learners*. Wellington: New Zealand Council for Educational Research (NZCER) Press.

Ofsted (2021), 'Research review series: history', www.gov.uk/government/publications/research-review-series-history/research-review-series-history

Olusoga, D. (2020), *Black and British*. London: Macmillan.

Pearson, J. (2012), 'Where are we? The place of women in history curricula'. *Teaching History*, 147, 47–52.

Phillips, R. (1998), *History Teaching, Nationhood and the State: A Study in Educational Politics*. London: Continuum International Publishing.

Quigley, A. (2018) *Closing the Vocabulary Gap*. Abingdon, Oxon: Routledge.

Richards, H. (n.d.), 'The surprising story of Henry Tudor', www.loom.com/share/b1697ef6787d491d9d005f94b573709e

Richards, H. (2017), 'Telling stories and teaching history', Huntington Research School, https://researchschool.org.uk/huntington/news/telling-stories-and-teaching-history

Riley, M. (2008), 'Into the Key Stage 3 history garden: choosing and planting your enquiry questions', *Teaching History*, 99, 8–13.

Rosenshine, B. (2012), 'Principles of instruction: research-based strategies that all teachers should know'. *American Educator*, 36, (1), 12–19, 39.

Sanghera, S. (2021), *Empireland: How Imperialism has Shaped Modern Britain*. London: Penguin.

Schama, S. (2000), *A History of Britain: At the Edge of the World? 3000 BC–AD 1603*. London: Penguin.

Schank, R. C. and Abelson, R. P. (1995), 'Knowledge and memory: the real story', In R. S. Wyer Jr. (ed.), *Knowledge and Memory: The Real Story*. Hillsdale: Lawrence Erlbaum Associates, pp. 1–85.

Sherrington, T. and Caviglioli, O. (2020), *Teaching WalkThrus: Five-Step Guides to Instructional Coaching*. London: John Catt, Hodder Education.

Snelson, H., Lingard, R. and Brennan, K. (2012), '"The best way for students to remember history is to experience it!" Transforming historical understanding through scripted drama', One Big History Department, Historical Association, https://onebighistorydepartment.files.wordpress.com/2018/01/scripted-drama.pdf

Snelson, H., Lingard, R., Holliss, C. and Boyd, S. (2023), *A new focus on...British Social History, c. 1920–2000 for KS3 History: Experiences of Disability, Sexuality, Gender and Ethnicity*. London: Hodder Educational.

Stevens, E. (2022), *40 Ways to Diversify the History Curriculum*. Carmarthen: Crown House Publishing.

The Sutton Trust (2011), 'Improving the impact of teachers on pupil achievement in the UK – interim findings' www.suttontrust.com/our-research/improving-impact-teachers-pupil-achievement-uk-interim-findings

Townsend, D. (2020), 'Jaws and the Peasants' Revolt: what history teachers need to know about storytelling', *Long Trail: Thoughts on the Teaching of History*, https://longtrailwinding. wordpress.com/2020/05/14/jaws-and-the-peasants-revolt-what-history-teachers-need-to-know-about-storytelling

VanSledright, B. A. (2002), 'Confronting history's interpretive paradox while teaching fifth graders to investigate the past'. *American Educational Research Journal*, 39, (4), 1089–115.

Wiliam, D. (2013), 'Principled curriculum design', Redesigning Schooling 3, SSAT (The Schools Network), https://webcontent. ssatuk.co.uk/wp-content/uploads/2020/03/20105155/ Redesigning-Schooling-3-Principled-curriculum-design-Dylan-Wiliam.pdf

Willingham, D. (2004), 'The Privileged Status of Story', AFT, https://www.aft.org/ae/summer2004/willingham

Wilson, F. (2012), 'How my interest in what I don't teach informed my teaching and enriched my students' learning'. *Teaching History*, 146, 52–6.

Wineburg, S. S. and Wilson, S. M. (1988) 'Peering at history through different lenses: the role of disciplinary perspectives in teaching history'. *Teachers College Record*, 89, (4), 525–39.

Young, M. (2013), '"Powerful knowledge": to what extent is this idea applicable to school geography? Bringing knowledge back in', Institute of Education, www.youtube.com/watch?v=r_S5De naj-k)

Index